Advance Praise for *The First L*

"This is the most powerful tool I've encountered for eradicating the problem of sexual harassment in the workplace. It provides a comprehensive view of the issue from all perspectives in a way any reader can appreciate, and it belongs on the shelf of every risk manager, executive, human resource professional, and employee."

Adriana Metcalf
Senior Vice President, Aon Risk Services

"This is a trail-blazing, insightful, and compassionate work on the psychosocial dynamics of sexual harassment. It will be of enormous value to anybody concerned with creating a more secure and humane workplace."

Ken Kressel, Ph.D.
Professor of Psychology and Director, Program in
Conflict Management, Rutgers University

"The First Line of Defense is a real breakthrough. For the first time, we are given an understanding of how sexual harassment begins and how we can create a workplace that reduces the risk that it will occur."

Linda Lamel, Esq.
Former Executive Director, Risk Insurance &
Management Society and Former President,
The College of Insurance

"This volume is a masterful explication of the dynamics of sexual harassment, and the ways to prevent its occurrence in organizations. Dobrich and Dranoff break new ground in their in-depth study of sexual harassment issues. The book should be required reading for all who work in organizations. It is destined to become a classic in the field."

James S. Wulach, Ph.D., J.D.
Director, Graduate Program in Forensic Psychology,
John Jay College of Criminal Justice, CUNY

The First Line
of
Defense

A Guide to Protecting Yourself
Against Sexual Harassment

WANDA DOBRICH
STEVEN DRANOFF

JOHN WILEY & SONS, INC.

NEW YORK • CHICHESTER • WEINHEIM • BRISBANE • SINGAPORE • TORONTO

ISBN 0-471-35358-2

Printed in the United States of America.

10 9 8 7 6 5 4 3 2 1

To our families
Marino, Ted, Johanna, and Oliver
and
Geralyn, Erik, and Kevin
without whose inspiration, patience, and support
this work would not have been completed.

FOREWORD

Sexual harassment in the workplace is a very serious problem in the United States. Claims of this sort increasingly land management personnel and companies in court to answer lawsuits brought by employees who allege that they are victims of conduct that constitutes sexual harassment. The stigma of the problem can ruin a career, lead to divorce, and inflict years of financial problems on management personnel and their companies.

Training in appropriate workplace behavior to avoid sexual harassment is a key focus of intense concern by corporations and management personnel. As a lawyer specializing in employment law and practicing at Baker & McKenzie, the world's largest law firm, I have been involved in creating and administering training programs for over two decades on these topics. This experience confirms that the time and effort which corporations expend to train their workforces on appropriate workplace behavior and in avoiding sexual harassment is a critical investment in workers, the company, and their collective productivity. Every dollar spent in training pays exponential dividends in terms of the risks and exposures that are avoided: costly lawsuits, a drain in management time diverted away into litigation, and the loss in productivity accompanying workplaces that are not marked by respect, dignity, and fairness to all employees.

The training philosophies and methodologies created by Wanda Dobrich and Steven Dranoff represent some of the most creative and cutting edge thinking on avoiding sexual harassment in the workplace. The core of that training philosophy is encapsulated in this book. Human resource managers, corporate counsel, risk managers, chief financial officers, and all right-minded individuals are well-served to use this book as a primer on how corporate America should view sexual harassment training. The philosophies and strategies in this book on training are time-tested, proven ideas that have worked for executives and supervisors at big and small companies alike.

In 1998 and 1999, the U.S. Supreme Court issued rulings in employment discrimination cases which indicate that corporate compliance and training programs are more important than ever before. Wanda and Steve's training programs are designed to fulfill corporate training needs recognized by the U.S. Supreme Court. The training program described in this book is unique in that it combines legal requirements and empirical data and observation from a psychological and scientific viewpoint to deliver a practical and usable method of preventing sexual harassment problems arising in any workplace. The groundbreaking research and training methodologies that form the core of Wanda and Steve's work are unique. This text is sure to become a standard guide in any corporate library and on all human resource professionals' shelves.

GERALD L. MAATMAN, JR.
Partner, Baker & McKenzie

Chicago, Illinois
January 2000

CONTENTS

Contents

INTRODUCTION

T his book is not like most other books that have been written about sexual harassment prevention. Most books start with
the actual sexual harassment and tell the reader what can be
done about it. Simply put, however, when we talk about trying
to STOP sexual harassment, we are already too late to PRE-
VENT it. Logic tells us that we cannot prevent something that
has already occurred. A discussion about prevention has to
start somewhere *before* the harassment event has happened.

There have traditionally been four lines of defense against
sexual harassment. The first line of defense is the individual.
When a harassed employee is able to deter or defuse a harassment encounter, it can be stopped without external intervention. When the parties involved fail to resolve their problem,
however, the second line of defense kicks in—the corporation.
Through its antiharassment policy, complaints can be addressed and remedies sought. If the corporation fails to stop a
harassment problem, the third line of defense kicks in—the
courts. An aggrieved employee can seek redress through litigation. When all else fails, the employer has available a fourth
line of defense—the insurance company. The corporation can

protect itself from economic harm by purchasing employment practices liability coverage that protects against sexual harassment claims.

In this country, we have focused almost exclusively on the second, third, and fourth lines of defense—the corporation, the courts, and the insurers—all but giving up on the individual. We have been in a crisis mode, trying to eliminate the problem of sexual harassment by encouraging people to rout it out, in one way or another, on its every showing. We encourage employees to come forward and complain if it occurs, we tell companies to tighten their policies and procedures that prohibit its occurrence, we ask the courts to litigate its occurrence, and we pay the insurers to underwrite its occurrence.

Does any of this effort *prevent* harassment? Again, we can't prevent something that has already occurred.

We have heard arguments that there is nothing else we can do. Enough is enough! Employees are tired of being admonished for their behavior or being warned, "Don't do that." Employers are tired of being held liable for the actions of certain employees who fail to "follow the rules." The laws to protect against the few "bad apples" inhibit and stifle the legion of the innocent. In point of fact, most employees are not, and never will be, "sexual harassers."

Those few "bad apples" who are resistant to change will just have to learn the hard way. The "school of hard knocks" is a painful experience for achieving social reeducation in the workplace, but, in the long run, after enough years of punishment, everyone will finally get the message. A peace treaty can then be formalized that redrafts the lines of communication in the workplace.

As psychologists, however, we doubt that scenario's supposed effect. We know instead that while punishment may push unwanted behavior underground, it stays there only for the moment. It is likely to resurface at another time—perhaps in another place, or in another form—because the motivation that underlies unwanted behavior does not disappear when we prohibit its surface expression in a particular instance. Punishment is not an effective means to *change* behavior.

We have another way of looking at the problem of sexual harassment.

We have already asserted that the prevention of sexual harassment must start *before* it has already occurred. To help us "find the beginning" of sexual harassment, we share with you our experiences during our ten years of training industry in sexual harassment prevention. We have asked employee groups across the country, "When does sexual harassment begin?" This turns out to be a most intriguing question.

The answers we are offered again and again by employees focus on defining harassment *acts:* Harassment begins when one employee demands sexual favors from another on threat of loss of employment benefits, or when the harasser overtly says or does something offensive and provocative to the victim. These are logical responses.

We have argued instead that a particular workplace interaction is "sexual harassment" psychologically only when one of the parties has identified it as such. "Sexual harassment" is a legal term, not a "human" term. "Suspect" workplace interactions go on all the time, but only sometimes do they fulminate in what we label sexual harassment at some point down the road. The "human conditions" are met long before the labeling as "sexual harassment" occurs.

Prevention therefore rests in gaining a better understanding of these workplace interactions. Time moves very quickly in human communication, and decisions are made about what employees can expect from one another on the job. Sexual harassment "contracts," as we call them, are forged with alarming speed, and they are made on the basis of both concrete work-role expectancies and personality factors. It is not at all unusual for harassed employees to report feeling that they "did not know" what was happening in the beginning and "could not stop" the communication until it was "too late."

We reasoned that if we could alter the course of these potentially "sexually harassing moments," we could go a long way to averting a problem.

But we needed a method to "slow the speedboat" in order to help people learn the skills that would protect them from entering a harassment contract. As psychologists, we know that the best way to find out about human behavior is to study it as it naturally occurs. In developing our theory, therefore, we constructed a simulated sexual harassment video drama as the stimulus for discussion, so that we could break the harassment experience down into its component parts.

We also used this simulated drama in our laboratory, to study the perception of sexual harassment by "untrained" observers. By analyzing how people actually perceive sexual harassment, we learned some rather surprising things about human beings. These insights are incorporated in our training and are presented throughout this book.

The contents of our simulated video drama are shown in story form in this book. Each chapter unfolds a sequence of events, beginning with the first day of employment of one of the harassment protagonists. You will meet the sexual harasser and study the developing harassment problem in the corporation in relation to his interactions with two colleagues, one a subordinate and the other a manager of equal rank. You will also gain an appreciation of the effect of the sexual harassment on others in the corporation, including coworkers and executive management who must all eventually cope with the harassment events.

The simulated drama is not unusual in any way. Rather, it is quite typical of the real sexual harassment episodes we have encountered in industry. It is nothing outside of the "ordinary fare" of sexual harassment. But, surprisingly, employees in training do not initially believe this. It has been our experience instead that any discussion of sexual harassment brings to the fore an enormous amount of resistance.

This resistance can take many forms. No matter how many times we tell people that the events they are about to see are "real-life," we inevitably hear the same defensive reactions: "No one would do this!" "We don't have this problem here!" "He's too obvious!" "She should fight back!" "No one acts like that anymore!"

Resistance is a ubiquitous thing. You will see it in all of its disguises throughout this book.

We next lift the screen from the protagonists to allow you to see what lies behind their interactions. After each chapter of the drama, we analyze the "rules" of sexual harassment that underlie the events, and the motivations of the characters who must measure their behavior against these standards. You will see that when the law and psychology drift too far apart, the potential for "sexual harassment" is quite high.

In our experience training in sexual harassment prevention, we have found that when people are able to "slow the speedboat" sufficiently, they can develop a deeper appreciation of the contribution of each player to the sexual harassment outcome. They are less riveted in laying blame and more focused on finding solutions.

Empathy for all of the protagonists in the sexual harassment drama is enhanced. Not to be confused with sympathy, empathy is the process that enables us to "know others from within" and to be socially related. As psychologists, we know that empathy is also our natural protection against sexual harassment. When we empathize with a person, however disapproving we may be of his or her surface acts, we are less likely to fear, aggress, or retaliate against that person.

Building empathy, however, takes work. It is not a passive process, especially for persons we judge harshly because of our upbringing, socialization, or life experience. Most of us do not naturally empathize with sexual harassers—or, for that matter, with their victims. Knowing nothing about the particular individuals involved, we do not instinctively "like" these people. These facts alone beg an explanation if we seek to strengthen our immunity to sexual harassment by building empathy.

The method in this book is to analyze sexual harassment step by step so that you can take a behind-the-scenes look and understand how the players got entrapped. You will see where the law and the corporation intrude in human relationships in the workplace. And, most important, you will see where other responses to one another might have caused the harassment entanglement to turn out differently.

In the final analysis, *you* are the first line of defense against sexual harassment. The better armed you are with insight into your biases, preferences, and empathy patterns, the better a protector you will be of yourself and your workplace.

The Hunter Becomes
the Hunted

$\mathcal{R}$ichard Whatman paced nervously, his hands clasped behind his back. The minutes passed slowly as he waited for the appointed hour to meet with the counselor from the Employee Assistance Program. Why did he ever agree to this intervention? At the time, he thought it a necessary concession to keep his job. But on second thought, what right did they have to demand this *too* of him?

With no time left to deliberate, Richard knocked on the door. If he had to be interrogated, at least he would not be accused of being uncooperative. The counselor opened the door and greeted him. She was younger than he had imagined. Quite a bit younger. What could she possibly understand about the complexities of his situation?

The counselor asked Richard in, and he sat opposite her. He defensively folded his arms across his chest in a combative posture. "I was told by Human Resources that as part of my rehabilitation, I will need to meet with you."

"Yes. My name is Dr. Wilhelm. Why don't you tell me what happened, in your own words."

Richard looked down. The room seemed strange and unfamiliar, and a feeling of unreality engulfed him. Nowhere in his experience had he been prepared for an inquisition such as this!

"Look, this is really embarrassing. I haven't figured it all out myself, yet. I have been accused of "—Richard stammered over the next two words—"*sexually harassing* a few of my office-mates." The phrase was spoken a bit too loud, as indignation replaced embarrassment. "But let me say at the get-go, *I* wouldn't call it that!"

Relying on a greater wisdom, the counselor did not respond to Richard's protestation.

"It *is* true that I said the things Human Resources put in that report you have there—or at least I remember *some* of them. But the *way* they are presented in your report—*that* isn't the way *I* remember them. When you take someone at their *literal word*, it's easy to mistake their intention."

Dr. Wilhelm braced herself for a tough interview. In a soft but firm voice, she asked, "What *were* your intentions, Mr. Whatman?"

"Maybe it's my sense of *humor* that was on trial," said Richard with growing annoyance. He realized that his tone was once again too harsh, and that this counselor would not believe him. Wanting to turn the interrogation around, he interjected a note of levity.

"Most of the statements in that report—I was only *joking around!*"

Richard's attempt at humor was a stretch. Feeling the tension, the counselor was silent, her expression impassive.

Spontaneous rescue by Dr. Wilhelm was not in the offing. Richard leaned in and tried once more to rid himself of this awful encounter.

"Listen. Between you and me, I'm a happily married man. Been with the wife for fifteen years. We have two beautiful children! I love my family! Why would I want to hurt them?"

"Getting back to what happened with your coworkers. . . ." The counselor's voice trailed off.

Richard noted with irritation that the counselor was not going along with his efforts at obfuscation. He ran out of patience. Richard was unable to contain himself a moment longer.

"This is *very* frustrating. Do you have any *idea* how political it is up there? Maybe I am in no position to be saying this, but did it ever occur to anyone that maybe, just maybe, these gals were angling to make *me* look bad?"

Dr. Wilhelm knew this was coming and was fully prepared.

"Do you have an idea how you got into this situation?" she asked.

Richard pushed himself to the back of his chair and cocked his head to one side. "No! Do you?" he queried defiantly.

Dr. Wilhelm suggested that, to understand how Richard's problem developed, they would have to start at the beginning.

CHAPTER ONE

We Teach Others
How to Treat Us

In the first chapter, you will see how the harassment couple forms and negotiates the first draft of the harassment contract, during the early period of engagement. This is the time when the harassment partners put forth the terms and conditions of the harassment relationship, implicitly or explicitly. Decisions are made quickly, and first impressions can be very hard to alter later on.

*C*rystal begins her employment at the American Corporation and is meeting her boss, Richard Whatman, on her first day as his administrative assistant. You are shown the sexual harassment drama from its beginning so that you can gain an appreciation of the importance of first impressions. In any introduction to a new colleague, much is communicated about who we are and how we expect to be treated.

A sexual harassment relationship between two employees usually develops over a period of time. Signposts of high risk for an eventual harassment outcome are always present early. How we react to these important cues can inform a potential harasser whether we are a "good candidate" for engagement. It is therefore helpful to devote some attention to exploring the dynamics of seduction into the harassment relationship.

THE SCENE

Crystal thought she must have been born under a lucky star. She landed an enviable job in the American Corporation, as the administrative assistant to Richard Whatman, a senior executive. With its century-old reputation, American was the bedrock of the city, the company others looked to for leadership and direction. This was not the kind of job Crystal thought she would be offered so soon after finishing business school. She had only worked in one other job before, in a much smaller professional accounting firm.

Whatever the source of her good fortune, Crystal accepted the job offer with gratitude and humility. The night before she was to begin work, Crystal was nervous. She hunted through her closet, searching for the *right* outfit to wear. She wanted to make a good impression—to look mature (for her 22 years), conservative (but not dull), and attractive (but not provocative). It was very important to make the *right* impression, not just a *good* impression. She was anxious to please yet uncertain about how.

Crystal did not permit herself to dwell long on this confusion. She pulled out a navy blue suit and laid it carefully across the back of the chair next to her bed. Before turning in for the night, she stretched out and spent a moment taking personal stock. Among her assets, she tallied an accepting nature, an accommodating disposition, and a pleasing personality. She also had a strong work ethic and was dependable, responsible, and organized. People usually took a liking to her. Comforted by these thoughts, Crystal eventually drifted off to sleep.

Richard Whatman arrived for work early on Monday morning and found three emergency messages already on his voice mail. The city never sleeps! It seemed awfully cold in the building. Were they now trying to save money on the heat, he wondered? Life in American had changed radically during his 15-year tenure in the corporation, especially after the merger. Richard mourned daily over the loss of the good old days. This was a bad habit of his; the better part of him knew quite well that the good old days were not so good, really. If they had been, the merger probably would not have been necessary.

American had taken some pretty big hits in the years prior to reorganization. No longer a bastion of prosperity and stability, the company had to adapt to change in order to survive.

The merger joined American with a foreign entity. Leadership was largely abroad, and only a few executives were transplanted to American soil. Much of the old administration of American had left, through downsizing or buyouts. Thus, while *little* had changed on the surface of doing business, *everything* was different in other ways. The autonomy Richard had once enjoyed had all but dried up.

Of course, Richard had been assured that the merger would not result in his losing his job. That was true enough. He was a big producer and had become accustomed to the many privileges that go along with success. However, the stakes were high. Some days, he felt as though he had to perform what seemed like miracles to impress his new superiors. There were no sacred cows anymore. Lacking many of the comforts the old American had afforded him, Richard had to do more with less.

Sorting through his correspondence, Richard found what he was looking for. He was due to meet with Liz, a fellow manager, and Griggs, American's CEO, to report progress on the Redman account. With the holidays past, he had no more excuses for delay. Redman was a new client that Richard and Liz were jointly cultivating and trying to court away from their competitor. If the Redman account performed well, it would galvanize Richard's reputation with the new regime. If not, he did not want to think about what the consequences would be.

Richard scanned the Redman documents in preparation for the meeting with Griggs. He was acutely aware of the potholes in his treatment summary and was hedging his bets that Griggs would be too preoccupied to scrutinize Richard's account. This was not the way Richard liked to do business with the CEO, but he had no choice. Redman was not going to move any faster, Liz was breathing down Richard's neck, and Griggs had called the meeting for *today*.

God, it was cold in here! Trying to put the Redman meeting out of his mind for the moment, Richard swiveled around in his chair to attack the next order of business for the day. At any moment, Crystal, his new administrative assistant, was due to report for her first day of work.

Richard had interviewed Crystal after Human Resources had screened her. She seemed to fit the job description. Goodness knows he needed all the office help he could get. The last two girls hadn't worked out. Both quit. How disappointing! It took time to break in a new girl, and Richard felt quite sorry for himself for having to do so with such frequency. This was just another example of the many obstacles he had to surmount just to hold his place in this company.

Nine o'clock, and, as Richard guessed, Crystal reported promptly to his office, right on time.

"Crystal, come in. Welcome to the American Corporation. I'm glad to see that Human Resources sent you back here. I had hoped they would. You know, I need a real crackerjack Gal Friday here—to keep me on target."

Crystal stood opposite Mr. Whatman's desk. She was a bit taken aback by his words. This was not at all what she had expected. Disarmed, she said nothing. She soon regained her composure.

"At your service, Mr. Whatman!" said an overly cheerful Crystal. She decided to ignore Mr. Whatman's remarks, as she did not know for certain what they meant. Crystal wanted to put her best foot forward.

"Where do I start?" she asked.

Richard paused and leaned back in his chair, taking it all in. He was oddly at peace with Crystal and happily surprised to find her so easy to get along with.

Crystal felt awkward. She was self-conscious. She was still standing opposite Mr. Whatman's desk because he had not offered her a seat. His gaze intimidated her, and Crystal could feel his eyes on all of her as she stood in his full view.

Finally, he spoke. "Please, call me *Richard*." His voice was mellow.

Mr. Whatman did not take notice as Crystal instinctively drew back.

"You will be responsible for all correspondence coming out of my office—mail, reports, annual budgets—*all of it*." This last phrase was drawn out.

He continued, "I understand you have excellent keyboarding skills. Know how to use a spreadsheet?"

Amused at his own subtle play on words, Richard looked at Crystal expectantly and wondered whether she had gotten his double entendre.

Crystal nodded *yes* to Mr. Whatman's question about her skills. But she did not know how to proceed with his confusing tone. She did not remember Mr. Whatman being this way. During their first meeting, before she was hired, he had seemed quite different—charming, almost. Acknowledging to herself how nervous she sometimes gets when meeting new people, especially people who are in authority or who command respect, Crystal decided that her discomfort was probably exaggerated.

"You will be responsible for all of my *personal* office needs."

Mr. Whatman looked approvingly at Crystal, thinking to himself that luck may have finally come his way in the form of this receptive, open-minded, young administrative assistant. Not at all *un*attractive, either! What an improvement over the last two girls he had had to suffer through.

Crystal felt her body shudder imperceptibly. A fleeting, quizzical expression crossed her face. With composure rapidly draining, she fought to regain self-confidence. The last thing she wanted was for Mr. Whatman to see her stumble.

"I, I, I was the administrative assistant at Kolar, before coming here. They had a pretty complicated network, so I don't think yours should give me too much trouble. I know some of it already!" Crystal laughed nervously.

She might even have a good sense of humor, Richard thought. What a coup!

"Excellent, excellent. We need someone like you around here. A sharp cookie with a good attitude!"

Crystal's smile faded, but Mr. Whatman did not seem to notice. Delighted with his new find, Richard visually examined Crystal, trying to take in the fine points about this new assistant.

"Yes, sir, Crystal, you and I should get along just fine. We will be working closely together over the next few weeks, until you get your feet wet." Richard grinned with satisfaction at this first encounter.

Just then, the telephone rang, signaling Richard to report to his meeting with the CEO. He excused himself and left a bewildered Crystal to set up her new workstation.

THE DIAGNOSIS

Crystal's tale is a case study on quid pro quo sexual harassment. This is the first form of sexual harassment identified by federal law. It occurs when submission to sexual favors is used as a condition of employment. Quid pro quo literally means *this for that*. Employment benefits are offered in exchange for sexual favors. It is also called *supervisor harassment*; only those in authority are in a position to manipulate the conditions of employment. Because this form of sexual harassment is most easily identified, some people think that it is therefore most easily stopped. Unfortunately, this is not the case.

We have shown a video of this opening scene between Richard and Crystal to hundreds of employees as part of our training in sexual harassment prevention. We have asked: Is there something about Crystal and Richard that marks them as prime candidates to become a quid pro quo sexual harassment couple?

People typically respond by describing Crystal and Richard in characteristic ways.

A TALE OF
TWO CRYSTALS

People generally have one of two reactions to Crystal. The first is to focus on her youth and inexperience as an explanation for the quid pro quo outcome that this scene portends. Crystal is "Dorothy from Kansas!" These people take pity on her plight. They remark that it is against Crystal's basic nature and family background to stand up to a senior authority figure in the workplace—especially a man, in a first encounter. They argue on behalf of her innocence; she wants to make a good impression, and she is unsure of Mr. Whatman's intentions. They assert that Crystal is not wrong to be conservative and give the relationship a chance before jumping to conclusions.

This group thinks Crystal is justifiably *inhibited.*

Other people have a different take on Crystal. They are angry at her passivity in this terribly obvious situation. After all, Richard gives her plenty of opportunity to refuse his seduction if she does not welcome it. Instead, she pretends that she is unaware of his intentions, and she disregards her personal feelings of discomfort. These people feel betrayed by Crystal. They are unwilling to forgive and excuse Crystal her ineffectiveness, even though she is young and naïve. They exhort her to *do something.*

This group thinks Crystal is unjustifiably *weak.*

A TALE OF TWO RICHARDS

Corresponding to the tale of two Crystals, people see Richard in one of two typical ways. Some view him with mock disapproval. They comment that he is "pathetic" in his attempts to make himself attractive to this younger woman. But they feel a certain empathy for him, nonetheless. He is competitive and under a lot of pressure from the reorganization of the company, so these people understand his misconduct as stemming from being overwrought by personal insecurity. Richard craves the bolstering that attention from women like Crystal potentially offers. While not condoning his acts, they describe him as "clueless."

This group thinks Richard is just a *buffoon*.

Other people see Richard as far more cunning and manipulative, and they construe his motives as more pernicious. They react to Richard with enormous disgust. His attempted seduction of Crystal overwhelms them, and they turn away from Richard entirely. They state that there is absolutely no excuse for him, and Richard should be fired, punished, demoted—and a few other choice consequences that shall go unnamed—for his unconscionable behavior.

This group thinks Richard is a serious *villain*.

These prototypes of Crystal and Richard are universal. All people voice them, like clockwork, every time we train. No matter who is in the group—supervisory or nonsupervisory employees, men or women, in manufacturing or professional companies—these twin tales of Crystal and Richard will emerge.

The riddle is: How come everyone *sees* the same acts, but *perceives* them in these different but *predictable* ways?

The answer to this riddle is not simple. We will return to it again and again throughout this book because it captures the essence of what needs to be understood to prevent sexual harassment. The subtle interplay between perception and cognition, fact and act, and the law and psychology, determines how we react to sexual harassment.

Curious about why people choose to see Crystal and Richard in one or another of these four typical ways, we invited observers into our laboratory to view a video of this same scene between Richard and Crystal. We then asked them to rate their perceptions of the characters, just as our employees do in training.

Not surprisingly, the observers also characterized the Crystal victim as either *inhibited* or *weak*, and the Richard harasser as either a *buffoon* or a *villain*. The same video events were shown to everyone, but people came to different conclusions about the characters, based on their own personalities and life experiences.

We then showed the observers subsequent scenes of Crystal and Richard. Once an interpretation of the prototype was made, however, it endured across all subsequent events involving that person. Once pegged a particular type, always that type. For example, even when our video Crystal eventually spoke up to her harasser, the perception of "inhibition" or "weakness" persisted.

What does this imply about how we form impressions about sexual harassment?

Our perceptions about victims and harassers become fixed early, and although we admit that a person's *behavior* can change when we are given new information to indicate as much, our ideas about underlying *character* are not easily altered.

Based on our observations, we would hypothesize that the process of character perception of harassers and victims might go like this. People form judgments about *character* based on observations of harassment *events*. We then interpret these observations based on our own *personalities* and *experiences*, and an impression of the harasser and victim is formed. Once decided, however, subsequent acts do not readily alter our initial impression of fundamental character.

But there is more to come.

You will remember that people opted for one of two interpretations of the victim and the harasser. We now also learn that the observers were not making judgments about the harasser and victim in isolation to one another. Rather, they seemed to be making assumptions about the motivations of each, based on observations of their reactions to one another.

For instance, when a person interpreted the victim as "inhibited," the corresponding harasser was almost always perceived as a "villain." Similarly, when the person interpreted the victim as "weak," the harasser was usually perceived as a "buffoon." People were looking at the harassment *pair* as a unit, not as individual players.

Fascinating! Who would think that we judge the character of the *victim* based on how he or she reacts to the *harasser*? And vice versa for the harasser?

Hence our term, the *harassment couple*. We are taking too narrow a view of sexual harassment if we look only for behavioral predictors of harassers or victims in isolation. Our observers inform us that the whole of the harassment relationship is equal to more than the sum of its parts. Sexual harassment is predicted by the *interaction* of the two protagonists, not by either one alone.*

---

*We must point out that there are most certainly instances in which a person forces sexual advances absolutely and unequivocally on another, against that person's wishes. However, this constitutes sexual assault, not sexual harassment.

We will explore the psychology behind these interactions as we go on. For the moment, let us summarize what we have learned so far about how first impressions are formed:

🖋 Judgments about the fundamental character of the harasser and victim are formed early in the relationship. Later information can alter the degree to which we see a person as having one or another characteristic, but we do not easily modify our basic impressions of people.

🖋 Impressions about character are based mutually on direct *observations* of the person and on our *interpretation* of those observations. Two people may form entirely different impressions about the fundamental character of a harasser and a victim, even though they have seen the same events.

🖋 Impressions of a harasser and a victim are formed based on their interaction with one another. Sexual harassment is seen from its beginning as an *interpersonal*, not an *individual*, problem. Neither the harasser nor the victim alone might form the harassment bond, were not the other a "right match."

People evaluate sexual harassment as a dynamic interaction between two employees. This dynamism is cast early in the relationship and is unlikely to change in kind, once judgment gels.

This is the power of first impressions.

If you have read carefully, you will have noticed that the basis for making judgments about sexual harassment is both *objective* and *subjective.* Every step of the way, from the beginning of the engagement period and courtship of the harassment partner to the eventual dissolution of the harassment "marriage," the subtle interplay of intellect and emotion, event and reaction, predicts the harassment outcome.

We will see further that this interplay of intellect and emotion is reflected in the collisions between the *law* on sexual harassment, which informs on harassment *acts,* and the *psychology* of sexual harassment, which informs on the perception of harassment *actors.* Both are necessary, but neither alone is sufficient to explain a sexual harassment outcome.

It is not enough to know the "rules" of acceptable workplace behavior. Nor is it enough to know how we "feel" about sexual harassment. We need to understand how *feelings* impact on intellectual *understanding* of events, and, conversely, how *understanding* the do's and don'ts shapes *feelings.*

The *prevention* equation is really quite simple. We have found, from extensive experience as consultants to industry and from our laboratory observations on the perception of sexual harassment, that when the law and psychology drift too far apart, the risk for sexual harassment increases.

THE PRESCRIPTION

Let us see how the diagnosis applies to Crystal and Richard. Taking a look first at the psychology of their interaction, it is not too difficult to see that Mr. Whatman's treatment of Crystal is inappropriate, provocative, and disrespectful. He does not invite her to sit down, putting her immediately in a submissive role. He uses demeaning language, referring to her as a *crackerjack Gal Friday*. He asks to be called by his first name, speaks in double entendre, and uses seductive innuendo. And all that in only the first five minutes of their exchange!

Crystal doubts herself and lets Mr. Whatman take the lead in their communication. She answers his questions to the best of her ability. She hopes that an impression of competency will surmount inner turmoil. Crystal does not trust her judgment sufficiently to step forward and take a stand when she is confused by Mr. Whatman. She turns against herself and in so doing leaves herself vulnerable to his whim.

In forming these first impressions of one another, Richard and Crystal begin negotiations on what is to become their harassment contract. How do they each specify the terms and conditions?

Richard has invited Crystal to collude with him. In the first draft of their sexual harassment contract, however, Richard has not yet specified concrete *quid's* to be exchanged for her *quo's*. Rather, he is tooling the relational boundaries of their deal, bit by bit, with her implicit consent. He wants to see how far he can push with Crystal, and she hasn't drawn a line in the sand.

This sexual harassment contract is based on the *affective* information the harassment couple share about one another in their beginning encounter. The "facts" of the case thus far would not constitute legal grounds for sexual harassment.

Absent legal justification, however, our psychological reaction to this scene is intense. Richard's treatment of Crystal stirs up a great deal of negative emotion in most people.

The *psychology* of this encounter takes precedence over the *law*. Recall that our laboratory observers rather quickly forgot what they "saw" of the harassment events but retained what they "felt" about it when making judgments about the characters. Similarly, you may have already formed a strong impression of Crystal and Richard based more on your own inner reactions to what you read than on the very limited information you have actually been given.

Richard and Crystal are not different from you. They too are penning a contract about what to expect from one another *based on nothing more than the kinds of affective impressions they have formed* on limited actual contact, but buttressed by much broader life experience.

The terms of this couple's harassment agreement are quite simple psychologically. Crystal will accommodate to Richard's needs, rather than expect him to make any adjustment to her. Richard will be demanding of Crystal, and she will comply in good cheer. Richard may express himself as he sees fit, and Crystal will not fight back.

And none of this is in their immediate grasp of awareness. Neither Richard nor Crystal explicitly *knows* that this is what is being communicated to the other, nor would either probably agree intellectually to these terms and conditions. Consciously, they both *know better*.

This harassment contract was negotiated on the *affective* level. Its terms and conditions were communicated indirectly through gesture, tone, use of words, and innuendo. On the *cognitive* level of *thought* or the concrete level of *act*, no harassment has yet occurred. Reread the dialogue between Richard and Crystal. Other than a few marginal utterances,

Richard's statements to Crystal are above reproach. Her responses to him are professional and appropriate.

But *affectively*, look at the mess they have already created! They're in the early stages of engagement. Richard thinks he has a green light for continued intrusion into Crystal's space. Crystal is worried, but she dismisses her better judgment in favor of her insecurities.

The harassment contract has been sealed.

Psychology and the law begin to drift dangerously apart. Nothing went wrong *legally* between Richard and Crystal yet, but everything is wrong *psychologically*. They have experienced a breach. Crystal and Richard are *thinking* one way about their business relationship but *feeling* another.

On what basis do you believe they will *act* in building a professional relationship?

We like to think of ourselves as rational beings who form impressions based on observation and who modify early hypotheses about character when subsequent experience teaches us otherwise.

Both of these assumptions are false, or at least untrue, when stated in the absolute. When it comes to highly charged relationships such as those that evolve into sexual harassment, our reactions often defy logic.

Identifying and correcting ruptures *when they occur* between the law and psychology—between fact and feeling, cognition and affect—is key to sexual harassment prevention. We can assure you that if Richard and Crystal do not repair the breach that has already occurred on first meeting, they mutually raise the threshold for a quid pro quo outcome.

There is good reason for the popular injunction: "Don't make a bad first impression."

First impressions are actually very accurate in predicting the quality of later relationships. More often than not, they are based less on fact than on affect. What Crystal communicates to Richard now will not be easily dispelled down the road without perhaps irreparable loss of trust between herself and Mr. Whatman, her new boss and harassment partner.

CHAPTER TWO

Bad Manners or
Sexual Harassment?

You will explore the first condition of hostile environment sexual harassment that unwelcome behavior is based on gender. The slope is slippery, however, when unwelcome aggression is tolerated in the boardroom but demands a different response when attached to gender at the office party. When the rules shift according to setting and player, it is difficult to act with confidence on your judgments about people.

*R*ichard leaves a confused Crystal and moves on to the next item on his busy agenda. He has a meeting with Liz, a manager of equal rank in the American Corporation, and Mr. Griggs, their mutual boss and the CEO of the company. The two managers have been partnered on the important Redman account. Richard grabs what he can to win a position of advantage over Liz in the meeting. He is professionally disrespectful and inconsiderate of Liz, who leaves the meeting upset.

In the second half of the chapter, Cathy, a third manager and office friend, joins Liz for an informal chat. Liz fills her in on Richard's inappropriate conduct at the office holiday party, where he exhibited much the same aggressiveness and inconsideration seen in the morning meeting. However, at the party, his misconduct was directed to numerous female colleagues. Is Richard's inconsideration in the CEO's office merely bad manners? Is his conduct at the holiday party a precondition for sexual harassment?

THE SCENE

Richard proceeded down the long hallway to the corner office suite. He became immediately conscious of the slightly warmer temperature of the air that brushed against his face as he swung open the double doors, crossed the portal, and entered the offices of Mr. Griggs, the CEO. The carpeting was thick underfoot, and the room had a musky scent whose source Richard was unable to identify. Was it the faint odor of the plumped leather sofas that formed an L-shape in the center of the room? Or, was it a faint trace of aftershave or cologne, absorbed by the walls and draperies and worn by the man who daily occupied this suite? Something about that odor signaled *importance* to Richard. He made a mental note to look into its source.

Capturing the attention of Rosy, Griggs's receptionist, Richard marked his presence with a firm nod of his head. Rosy acknowledged Richard with a return gaze that equaled Richard's cool indifference. No words passed between the two. Other than the steady hum of the computers and fax machines, no sounds were heard. The intercom buzzed, and Rosy spoke softly to her boss.

"Mr. Griggs will be with you shortly," said Rosy to Richard, who offered no reply.

Rosy sighed, thinking, "What a cold fellow that Richard is!" She had been employed by American for a long time and was quite used to the likes of Richard. In her mind, they were big producers who fancied themselves executives. Not wanting to trouble herself further with Richard, she turned away and continued with her work.

The reception area was brightly illuminated by the recessed high hats that evenly dotted the vaulted ceiling and by the sunlight that streamed through two solid walls of windows. At this height, 48 stories above the street, the city was a panorama that stretched as far as the eye could see. In this grand ambience, Richard momentarily felt himself to be very small. Fending off thoughts of intimidation, he seated himself on the leather sectional and scuffled through his Redman file, arranging the critical information in the precise order required for the morning presentation.

Just then, Liz bounded into the suite. She greeted Richard with a head nod and marched past the sectional directly to Rosy.

"Hi, Rosy," said Liz. Rosy smiled and leaned down to hand Liz a small package.

"Bill gave this to me to give you," said Rosy as she handed a small, wrapped gift box to Liz. "He told me to tell you he was sorry he couldn't give this to you personally, before his trip."

Liz knew the contents of the box and smiled in appreciation. "Bill told me he was leaving me this. He gave a holiday gift to all of his managers. Thanks, Rosy." Liz tucked the box in her briefcase.

"Mr. Griggs said he'd be available in a few minutes," said Rosy. "He's been in a bear of a mood this week because of the audit." Rosy leaned in and spoke to Liz in a hushed tone. "I'd watch out, if I were you!" she mockingly cautioned Liz.

"Really?" replied Liz, only half in jest. "Thanks for the warning!"

Liz turned to the couch where Richard had already seated himself. She noted his placement on the sectional and felt instant irritation. She recalled an article written by a psychologist on body language and what is communicated by physical proximity. Richard occupied the vertex of the angle formed by the L-shaped sectional. With his arms spanning the back of both sides of the sectional, Liz could not avoid sitting in close proximity to him, whichever arm of the couch she chose.

"Typical Richard," she thought. "Always finding a way to make his importance felt."

Richard had invaded Liz's "space" before they had uttered a single word to one another. Liz greeted Richard with a perfunctory "Hello" and sat as far away from him as she could.

"Are you worried?" Richard asked Liz.

The question provoked Liz for reasons she could not quite put her finger on. She did not answer Richard. She believed him to be less than sincere. In private, she reflected that indeed she was plenty worried.

She and Richard were skating on thin ice on this account. Liz appreciated that the Redman deal presented American with an important opportunity. Redman was a key player in the industry. If the recently merged American wanted to assert its place in the international market, what better way than to win Redman away from its competitors?

The new European leadership had recognized the possibilities for growth, and had placed a lot of pressure on Griggs to succeed in this mission. This pressure spilled down to Liz. She was no stranger to stress, having worked in the industry for nearly a decade, but the picture was still more complicated. In the "hot seat" to win the account, Griggs determined that, to improve his chances of victory, he would team Richard, his top producer, with Liz, who had a terrific way with people.

"Griggs fails to take into account that working with Richard is nearly *impossible!*" thought Liz with dismay.

Pooling talent did not always work when personalities clashed. Liz and Richard had little in common. Liz found Richard extremely competitive, and she could not trust him. He was not a team player. Richard found Liz too conservative. Besides, he did not like to share his thunder with anyone.

"As if that is not bad enough," thought Liz, "there is also the internal intrigue in Redman to contend with."

Over the course of meeting with Redman executives, Liz had uncovered news of an upcoming change in stewardship in the organization, as yet undisclosed to the public. She shared this confidence with Richard, and the two built a strategy: Strike while the iron is hot, and close a deal—perhaps a lesser one than they might otherwise accept—to get a foot in the door before the transition. To fail to bring a Redman contract home to Geneva would spell disaster for Richard and Liz, and they both knew it.

On the other hand, they knew full well that even a hard-won contract might be short-lived. The upcoming heir apparent to the Redman throne did not think as kindly of American as the present CEO and was very strongly committed, through personal ties, to a competitor. Liz did not know how much of this Griggs knew. Nor did she know how much of it Richard planned on sharing with him at the meeting that day.

The intercom buzzed again. Rosy ushered the two managers into the office of the CEO.

"I apologize that this meeting will be briefer than I had anticipated." Mr. Griggs looked up from behind his shiny mahogany desk. "I have a conference call coming from Geneva at 10 A.M.," Mr. Griggs declared as Richard and Liz entered the room. "Please sit down and let's get started."

Richard was relieved. There would be no time for close scrutiny of the record. Whew! Lady Luck was smiling on him!

"I am most concerned with this account. As you know, Charles Redman is a formidable influence in this industry. Geneva knows that too. Whichever way he goes, the rest will follow."

Usually the picture of confidence and poise, Mr. Griggs seemed uncommonly apprehensive. Richard did not wait a moment longer.

"I think you will be very pleased at the progress made on this client. I have everything you need here, sir," said Richard with aggressive assurance, hoping his one-page synopsis of the Redman account would please the CEO.

"What a creep!" Liz thought. Richard is acting as if *he* did all the work on the account! What about *her* contribution to the contract?

"As you can see, Mr. Griggs, these figures project that Redman will be on top of our client list by the end of next year," said a triumphant Richard.

Mr. Griggs scanned the record handed to him. He was obviously pleased. "How did you get Redman to come on board, Richard?"

With feigned humility, Richard replied, "Well, sir, they didn't want to buy into our concept at first. Charlie is extremely change-averse. We had to start slow."

"How did you do it, Richard?" asked an enlivened Griggs.

"It wasn't easy, sir, I assure you," boasted Richard.

"Excellent work!" Mr. Griggs finished scanning Richard's summary and turned to Liz.

"Do you have anything to add to this, Liz?" He looked expectantly at Richard's coworker for a response.

Liz knew Richard's tactics well. She berated herself for being taken off guard once again by his blatant self-promotion. Richard did not so much as mention any of the problems with the Redman account, including the fact that the *incoming* CEO had not been won over at all. *Small* detail that Richard overlooked.

"I too am pleased to have come this far with the account." Liz shot an angry glance in Richard's direction.

"And as for the projections for next year, I would agree with Richard that we can be . . . *hopeful.*" Liz was irritated and her gaze was fixed downward.

Mr. Griggs looked quizzically at Liz, not understanding her lack of enthusiasm about the obvious progress Richard reported. Before he could question her further, however, the buzzer signaled that his overseas call was on the line.

"Good work, both of you!" said Mr. Griggs hurriedly. "We'll continue this talk tomorrow." The CEO indicated the end of the meeting.

The two managers left the executive suite and walked down the hallway. Liz's attention drifted as Richard boasted about "the great job we did," and how fortunate they were that Griggs didn't have the time to thoroughly scrutinize the Redman account.

But Liz was in no mood for jubilation.

"What a great job *we* did?" thought Liz. "As for the great job *he* has done, a great *snow* job is more like it."

Richard and Liz parted ways at the elevator bank. Richard pressed the down button, to go to the executive cafeteria. Though it was close to lunchtime, Liz was not hungry. She went back to her office instead and closed the door, welcoming some quiet time to sort things out.

Liz was uncomfortable about what had just transpired, though she was not clear on what she should have done differently under the circumstances. Should she be like Richard and proclaim *her* successes? Self-exaggeration offended her. Should she have told Mr. Griggs the blunt truth about the Redman succession and engendered the wrath of her partner Richard by "snitching" on him? Does Griggs really care about "the truth" anyway, or would he rather hear good news until and unless it's absolutely necessary to know otherwise?

Liz was interrupted by a knock on the door. Cathy, her friend and fellow manager, asked to come in. The two women had come on board at American around the same time and had formed an immediate bond. This was unusual for Liz, who did not open up readily to many people.

Though conservative in her private life, Liz had grown to trust Cathy as a safe confidant when trying to negotiate the political waterways of corporate life. Liz would often test her impressions against Cathy, though she never admitted to relying on her friend in this way.

Liz opened the door with some relief. Cathy had been out sick and had only returned to work that day.

"So, how was the holiday party?" Cathy asked Liz.

"You should have seen him! Richard Whatman!" Liz rolled her eyes.

Cathy could feel her anger flash. She did not let on right away, however, wanting to give her friend a chance to talk.

"Lucky girl! You were out sick! Richie was sitting at our table, with the rest of the managers. And, let's say, he drank *a bit too much*." Liz drew out the last few words for added emphasis.

Liz knew Cathy pretty well. She suspected this last comment would rouse Cathy to the ready, and she wanted to see how her friend would react to this latest Richard story.

It worked. "What did he do *this* time?" asked Cathy, a trifle annoyed.

"His usual. He was all over me and a few of the other women, making outrageous remarks and putting his hands where they didn't belong. He was even worse on the dance floor!" Liz's face contorted into a grimace of remembered disgust.

"Not *again*." Cathy's annoyance was mounting. "He's too much. Someone oughta chain and muzzle him!"

Her intonation rising, she prodded Liz. "What did you do?"

"What *could* I do? I didn't want to make a big deal out of it, or make it more noticeable than it was already. How *embarrassing!*"

"Why not? You *know* how he gets. Why don't you just stop him?" Cathy paused expectantly.

Liz drew back in her seat in abject silence. She felt embarrassed. Cathy disapproved of her. "Maybe I *am* a coward," she thought.

A frustrated Cathy knew she wasn't getting through. She decided to take another route. "Liz, he's not your boss. There isn't *anything* he can do to you."

Liz was stone silent. Cathy finally snapped. "Boy, if it were me, I'd tell him a thing or two!"

Feeling misjudged and misunderstood, Liz challenged Cathy in return.

"If it's so simple, how come no one *else* stops him, either?"

THE DIAGNOSIS

The first condition of hostile environment sexual harassment is that unwelcome conduct is based on *gender*. Liz indicates that Richard's unwelcome sexually suggestive behavior at the holiday party was directed to numerous female employees. Uninvited and inappropriate touching, dancing, and verbal commenting were directed to particular employees on the basis of their being *women*. Had Richard's behavior been *hostile* but not directly *sexual*, the interpretation would have been the same, if *only female* employees were subjected to it. And if a woman had directed unwelcome and offensive behavior toward a *man*, solely on the basis of *gender*, the effect again would have been the same.

Sound simple? Liz doesn't find it so. What confuses her?

Although the *law* may single out particular instances in which *hostility* is also *harassment*, the very same behavior in another work context may simply be counterproductive or noncollegial, or in poor taste, but not *unlawful*.

There are many similarities psychologically between Richard's conduct toward Liz in the meeting with the CEO and at the office holiday party. In both instances, Richard is inconsiderate, disrespectful, self-serving, and maybe even pushy and obnoxious. These behaviors emerged in the business meeting. The very same adjectives might be used to describe Richard's provocative conduct at the office party.

Richard is the same *Richard* in both workplace scenes. But do we evaluate his behavior similarly in both contexts?

Some people may argue that Richard's behavior in the meeting with the CEO is not unlawful but is actually acceptable or even *expected* in competitive business practice. What makes a top producer successful? Certainly not passivity or putting the needs of others on a par with his or her own. An altruistic outlook is no algorithm for "closing the deal."

Richard may be in a quandary. Ways of conducting himself that are profitable in one context are unlawful in another.

Maybe Richard *should* know to change his behavior according to the setting, to avoid accusations of sexual harassment.

But the truth is that many of Richard's "hostile" qualities *benefit* his economic interests and those of the company. Therefore, it is unlikely that the law alone will compel Richard to change his behavior to accommodate Liz's emotions.

In fact, there are some industries that thrive because of employees with Richard's exact personality style.

In contrast, Liz does not stop Richard because it is not in her character to confront him head-on, whether his hostility is encountered on the dance floor or in the boardroom. Like Richard, she too is the same person in both contexts and makes the same choice to dodge aggression.

A strict interpretation of the law on gender-based hostility advises that Liz is on solid ground to do as Cathy suggests and stand up to Richard at the office party. Cathy would like to see her friend set an example by protecting herself and the *silent majority* of women at the office gathering who, like Liz, resent Richard's unwelcome advances.

Perhaps Cathy is right.

But ask yourself this: Should Liz do the same in Mr. Griggs's office? Should she protest to her superior that Richard's style of doing business is offensive to her and thereby hope to require Richard to stop?

This is a more ambiguous situation.

Stated another way, should Liz demand of herself that she become more assertive *here* but not *there,* even if confrontation does not come to her naturally, is not a part of her job description, and is not motivated by her own internal needs? Is she entitled to feel resentment that *she* should have to change in ways that are uncomfortable in order to accommodate to Richard's problem?

Liz is called to task in the scene with Cathy. The critical moment arrives when Cathy asks why Liz does not tell Richard off. Use the muscle of the law!

Liz withdraws from what she feels is criticism from Cathy, and she outwardly justifies her inaction on the basis that "No one else stops him either!"

This is an excellent observation. And it is one that, in our experience, runs "true to form" in many cases of coworker harassment.

The conflict deepens as the *should's* pile up. Richard *should* control himself. Liz *should* confront Richard. Cathy *should* support her colleague to stop sexual harassment. Crystal *should* set better boundaries. And the law says that employees *should* enact the *should's*. Everyone knows what he or she *should* do, but no one is doing it.

When psychology and the law drift too far apart, the risk for sexual harassment increases.

THE PRESCRIPTION

You have now met two potential sexual harassment couples in the early phase of engagement: Crystal and Richard in Chapter 1, and Liz and Richard in Chapter 2. Each of the women "knows" or at least "senses" that something is amiss, but neither has yet acted on that awareness.

Liz is describing Richard's hostility toward her at the office party. She writes it off to intoxication, even though she has had other dealings with him in the workplace that have also been marked by hostility.

Liz does not act.

Liz tells Cathy about the other women at the holiday party who were also targeted by Richard for hostile and unwelcome exchanges.

In a conspiracy of silence, the other women do not act.

Crystal experiences Richard's hostility. She is made extremely uncomfortable by the verbal and nonverbal cues she picks up from him during their first meeting.

Crystal does not act.

What accounts for the *in*action of *all* these different woman employees toward the same harasser?

Some people argue that it is easier to justify Crystal's inactivity because of her work situation. As Richard's administrative assistant, she is vulnerable to his harassment because of the power he holds over her employment.

Perhaps so. But Richard's authority over Crystal can also be a plus in the "Why doesn't the victim take action?" equation. Because quid pro quo sexual harassment involves conditioning of sexual advances to tangible employment benefits, it is measured by *acts.* It is concrete and demonstrable, and this is a psychological and a legal plus.

Abuse that is "subtle" can be harder to cope with psychologically and harder to demonstrate legally. In the case of Liz, Richard's coworker of equal rank, there is no concrete standard for judging the effect of his hostile acts on her work conditions. Liz is left to form her own judgment about whether Richard's behavior is sufficiently negative to constitute a detriment to her work environment.

Liz first has to separate her anger at Richard's "general hostility" and disrespectful treatment from her anger at his "harassing hostility" when his aggression is gender-based. This is a *legal* and not a *practical* distinction—and, emotionally, it is a tough call.

In the absence of a tangible standard, the opinions of others who also experience or witness the harasser's hostility take on great importance. No one has seen Richard with Crystal, but his hostility toward Liz, or at least some of it, is public.

This brings us to a second important difference between the harassment coupling of Liz compared to that of Crystal. Supervisor sexual harassment most often goes on behind closed doors. The sexual harassment is a "family secret" that is kept under wraps by the couple, usually for an extended period of time.

In contrast, in cases of coworker harassment, it is most common for others in the organization to *see* it. In Liz's case, we see the importance of coworkers in shaping the "home life" of the hostile environment sexual harassment couple. The conspiracy of silence we read about is a powerful deterrent against speaking out, especially for an employee such as Liz, who is not by nature confrontive. Pressure from Cathy to do something about Richard only makes matters worse.

Because *opinion* is so important in judging hostility that is based on *gender* (as opposed to hostility based on *abuse of authority*), we decided to explore how it is formed from the very beginning, before a relationship reaches the stage of bona fide sexual harassment.

We showed to observers the videos of only two of the scenes you have just read: Liz telling Cathy about Richard's hostility at the office party, and Crystal on her first day of work with her new boss. Neither woman confronts Richard in either of the two scenes. The observers knew considerably less than you do now, for they did not see Richard's aggressiveness in the meeting with Mr. Griggs or learn the background of his office competition with Liz.

We wanted to learn more about how these two women are perceived in relation only to gender-based hostility. More specifically, we wanted to learn whether employees "know" who will be "chosen" for engagement in sexual harassment, based on any cues given off by the victims.

We reasoned that if coworkers can pick out a victim, so can harassers.

We asked the observers to evaluate Liz and Crystal on dimensions of behavior that underlie *assertiveness*, commonly thought to be a natural antidote to becoming a harassment victim. Some of the traits that describe the characters include: "shy," "confident," "outspoken," and so on.

Looking objectively or literally at the scenes, there is little difference between the *overt* reactions of Liz and Crystal to Richard. Both women withdraw from confrontation when he displays hostility. Neither asserts a boundary or communicates dislike of hostile and inappropriate verbal remarks and innuendo.

With no other factual information available, the observers rated Liz and Crystal similarly. Neither was seen as strongly assertive. This was not surprising; it corresponded to the fact that neither woman "fought back."

But an interesting twist was encountered. You may recall the *Tale of Two Crystals*. Though they gave Liz and

Crystal superficially similar ratings for overall assertiveness, the observers perceived the two women quite differently in the particular clusters of traits that defined their behavior. Like film developing in a dark room, the observers formed impressions that differentiated Liz's nonassertiveness from Crystal's.

They did not know consciously that they were doing this, for they saw neither woman as more assertive than the other!

We found this fascinating. There was little superficial difference in Richard's acts toward these two women at this stage of the drama, but *subtle* differences in their *responses* to him were starting to shape the nature of their harassment contracts. And our observers picked up on these subtle nuances in character long before they became big differences in response to the harassment events.

If observers could pick up on these subtle cues in *less than four minutes* of videotape exposure, what do you think the women at the holiday party knew, within their "conspiracy of silence?"

More menacingly, what does Richard know?

An organization that is experiencing coworker sexual harassment is often a smoldering cauldron of these perceptions, many of which fall below the horizon of awareness in the early stages.

Let's summarize what we know so far about hostile environment or coworker sexual harassment:

- ❦ The hostility is gender-based. This is a moving target. As we have seen, the *same* hostility in a *different* workplace context may not be sexual harassment. Or, the *same* hostility, if delivered to a *different* employee, may not be sexual harassment.

🐦 The standard for the hostility itself is also a moving target. The perception of hostility, and not necessarily the tangible consequences of hostile acts themselves, constitutes an abusive environment.

Amid this ambiguity, we finally learn that employee reactions to coworker hostility are also murky. Different constellations of personality factors underlie assertiveness.

🐦 We may not explicitly know what these personality factors are, but coworkers and harassers alike are sensitive to them and read subtle cues long before the harassment occurs. These perceptions shape the future "home life" of the harassment couple in the corporation.

This last point is critical. In moving forward, we need to harness this awareness so that we can convert sensitivity into insight. Only then can we make choices when we're in situations that are ambiguous and are based only on perception rather than on fact.

CHAPTER THREE

Not All Acts of Hostility
Are Created Equal

You will learn what justifies identifying sexual harassment as a special case of workplace hostility. Early socialization experiences and personality style contribute to making some workers more vulnerable to workplace aggression than others. These differences can conflict with the social ideal of gender equity. We can't change socialization patterns to prevent sexual harassment, but we can teach men and women how to respond to aggression on the job in a way that fits their personality style.

$\mathcal{R}$ichard does not bask in his glory for too long, after his triumph with Griggs over the Redman account. He has a large appetite for success and is unable to rest easy until he secures a firm commitment from this troublesome client. Richard shares his frustration with Joe, a junior colleague. He bemoans the difficulty he has had, since the European merger, in holding his position as top gun in the corporation.

You have seen an inconsiderate Richard in relation to Crystal and Liz. You will now have the opportunity to study his character in relation to a male colleague. As he did with the women, Richard again writes off his work frustrations and disappointments as effects of the incompetence of others. This distortion is pervasive. Externalizing blame is a part of Richard's makeup. It permits him to target others in his line of vision for his perceived misfortune, thereby setting the stage for abusive behavior in the workplace. Does Joe differ from Liz, Cathy, or Crystal in his reaction to Richard's aggressiveness?

THE SCENE

Two months passed quickly for Richard after the first meeting with Griggs on the Redman account. The problem had grown more serious with time. The succession of the CEO was now imminent and, try though he did, Richard was unable to get the ear, much less the trust, of the heir apparent. Richard could not remember a time when he encountered such resistance in a client organization, especially one with so many seemingly mutual positives in the marketing equation. None of his usual tactics had worked in sustaining negotiations.

"This cannot be!" Richard thought. He pored over his meager record of the month's activity on the Redman account. He could not unravel why it had gone wrong.

Richard reached over the papers strewn haphazardly across his desktop and buzzed for Crystal on the intercom. He needed a distraction.

"Crystal," he said, "make a reservation in our regular place for lunch. I have some important news for you."

Richard stuffed the papers in his handsome attaché, a prop to lend a note of sophistication and importance to his image. He secretly wished to impress his young and not-too-unattractive administrative assistant during their lunch date.

"Crystal is the only bright spot on my calendar today," Richard sighed. He had to admit to himself that he felt lucky to have landed such a prize.

Richard's prospects were looking rather gloomy to him. When things did not go his way, he was prone to moodiness and melancholia. When his spirit was somber, half-formed images bobbed above and below the horizon of Richard's awareness. One vision involuntarily grabbed his attention.

"Stay out of the kitchen if you can't stand the heat!"

From his pulpit at the head of the dining room table, Richard's father's voice bellowed out in resonant oratory that carried his invective throughout the house. This was one of his few favored expressions, and he used it in generous measure against his son, ostensibly to build character. A young Richard would lower his head in humiliation, ashamed that he had once again been a disappointment to his father.

Richard dismissed this vision as quickly as it formed. He repeated quietly the rejoinder to the intruding emotion.

"Failure is not an option!"

It had become Richard's personal mantra in times of self-doubt. "I *can* take pressure. There will *be* no defeat. The victory of Redman belongs to *me*—one way or another!"

The clouds hung low, and the sky was a dark gray. A light rain had begun to fall. Richard wanted to feel good. He determined that this was a perfect time to cheer Crystal with news of his—no, hopefully, *their*—upcoming business trip to Las Vegas.

"I bet she's never been to Las Vegas." Richard felt quite magnanimous about his anticipated gesture. He would make her feel important by inviting her to accompany him as his special assistant. A splendid opportunity for her. Not so bad for him, either! And why not celebrate the invitation over lunch at Denny's Pub?

Richard got momentarily lost amid pleasant thoughts of the Vegas trip and a few "business" meetings with Crystal. He'd better tell her to pack day *and* evening clothes. Richard was mentally making plans.

Just then, Liz called Richard to tell him about her recent activity on the Redman account. She was nearly bursting with excitement as the words spilled out one after another. Richard mostly listened. He replied in monosyllabic and monotonic measures to his partner's lively cadence.

Richard was terribly annoyed by Liz's success.

"Does *Griggs* know that?" he grilled Liz in a menacing voice.

Liz indicated the affirmative. Richard slammed down the phone, uttering only a very curt goodbye to his colleague.

Or, was she his competitor, Richard wondered? Liz's success was an unwelcome twist of events.

Richard looked at his watch. He had a little time before his luncheon with Crystal, and he was suddenly restless. He needed air. Pacing the hallway, Richard saw Joe's door ajar. Fine! He will make conversation with this newly promoted junior manager. Richard suspected rightfully that Joe looked up to him and would welcome a congratulatory "Welcome aboard" speech from a senior manager of Richard's status.

Joe was a little over a decade younger than Richard. He was an ambitious man who took seriously the task of building his reputation and credibility in the corporation. He also took seriously the task of building his personal fortune. Joe had an acquired knack for reading the pulse of corporate politics, and he knew how to play people to his best advantage. He impressed others as open-minded, even-tempered, and low-keyed, but below the surface Joe was shrewd. He never took his eyes off the road.

Richard was correct in his assumption that Joe admired him, at least from afar: Joe had not yet had the opportunity to get close enough to Richard to know much about him firsthand. Having reached the junior management level, Joe sincerely hoped for the opportunity to work with Richard. Maybe he could learn a few of Richard's keys to success.

"Hey, Joe. Congratulations on your promotion." Richard sat down in the chair opposite Joe, who was stationed at his laptop.

"Thanks." Joe looked up and indicated a welcome to Richard.

Joe was surprised and flattered that Richard was paying him an informal visit. It was an acknowledgment to Joe that they were both members in the same "club."

"Things better start looking up, soon. I tell you, Joe, this department has too many problems. If I were the boss, I'd make a few changes around here. You betcha!"

Joe was taken aback by the tone and content of Richard's diatribe. He had not imagined Richard this way. He thought the sun and moon rose around this corporate star! And he assumed that Richard was as pleased with his position in American as others were envious of it.

Maybe he'd better listen carefully and follow Richard's lead. Joe would not show his surprise.

"Sure, Richard. I guess you're not the general—only a sergeant."

Joe's slight stammer belied the impression he was trying to create—that he was on the inside track and knew what Richard was alluding to.

Nothing could have been farther from the truth.

Richard was offended by Joe's remark. Richard did not consider himself a *sergeant* to *General* Griggs. This junior manager was naïve and had a few lessons to learn about Richard!

"That may be true—for *now!*" Richard said with authority. *This* star was still rising.

Joe was not sure where Richard was coming from, but he *was* sure that *something* he had said had agitated him. He'd better back down until he gained sure footing.

"You shouldn't let things get you so uptight, Richard. You'll give yourself an ulcer."

Joe was reaching for a safe, innocuous remark. But as soon as he had made this statement, he sensed that he had missed the mark. Richard was not comforted. He blistered.

"The insolence!" Richard thought. He set to pacing the perimeter of Joe's office.

For an instant, Joe thought Richard resembled a caged tiger.

"If these gals can't do what they are *supposed* to, I say A-D-I-O-S! We'd all be better off!"

Richard threw his hands up for emphasis.

"*Gals?*" thought Joe. "Who refers to people that way? Why single out the women?"

Joe was liking this conversation less and less, but he dared not ask Richard what he was getting at.

Richard was still maintaining a furious pace. His mind wandered away from Joe. He couldn't stop thinking about Liz and the positively *treasonous* steps she had taken with Redman. Was she trying to make *him* look bad?

"Failure is not an option," Richard reminded himself.

The mantra snapped Richard back to attention. He stopped pacing and turned to Joe, whom he had left hanging in mid-conversation, and picked up where he had left off.

"Instead, Mr. Griggs lets *some* people get away with *murder!* I just don't understand that guy. If I had all of *his* power, you can bet things'd be different!"

Joe was stumped. He was more puzzled now than when the conversation with Richard began, and his discomfort gave way to irritation. Although he could not decipher Richard's cryptic communication, Joe suspected he was somehow being put in the middle of something he neither liked nor understood.

"Sure, Richard, heads would roll. I'd watch it, though. Griggs is the CEO, and one day it might be your head that he's after."

Joe was still trying to be friendly.

Richard gathered himself up and left. It was time for lunch with Crystal.

THE DIAGNOSIS

Sexual harassment is considered to be a *special* case of workplace aggression. It is hostility that is directed against an employee on the basis of *inclusion in a protected class*—in this case, *gender*. Federal law, under Title VII, prohibits it.

Richard hurts many employees (and perhaps even some clients) with his disrespectful behavior. Earlier, we saw Liz and Crystal struggle against Richard's hostility. Now we see Joe struggle. Some of Richard's expressions of hostility are treated as bad manners and are punishable only by conscience; others are labeled sexual harassment and are punishable by law.

Is this distinction rational?

The Supreme Court would consider it so. Why? What is *different* about Richard's abusiveness toward Joe as compared to his treatment of Liz? Or of Crystal?

Two concepts come into play in discerning what is so *special* about sexual harassment and why the courts have determined that it is a unique form of discrimination, unlike other expressions of inconsiderate behavior. Its origins are to be found in our early *socialization* experiences and our unique *personalities*. Each makes an important contribution to how we conduct ourselves as men and women, both in our private lives and in the workplace.

Socialization begins at the start of life. Children are taught what it means to be a man or a woman in the adult world. Parents, teachers, and peers contribute significantly to the formation of gender identity.

Although there are some differences in the definition of what is "womanly" or "manly" among different cultural groups, there are many more common characteristics that most of us would agree are "typical." These typical characteristics form cultural *sex role expectancies*—ways in which women *expect* to be treated by men, and men by women.

Personality is the second factor contributing to how we define ourselves as men or women. Even within broad generalizations about sex role expectancies, the way we act is based on our unique upbringing and life history.

For instance, Liz may be passive because of the way she experienced aggression when she was growing up. Crystal may be accommodating because her family rewarded her for pleasing others. Joe may have learned that surface charm will win him the trust he requires in order to satisfy his ambition.

Within the range of all behaviors defined as "masculine" or "feminine," we pick and choose those that fall within our comfort zone, based on our personal history.

The need for antidiscrimination law derives from the interplay between these *socialization* universals and individual *personality* differences. Culturally defined gender roles predispose women to a greater likelihood of sex discrimination than men in the workplace.

This is old news. Men have traditionally dominated the world of work, and though the landscape is changing, women still do not have equal access to positions of leadership.

Simply put, sexual harassment involves an abuse of power, and women generally have less of it. The statistics on sexual harassment leave little room for doubt that it is still largely a "women's problem," though this may become less true over time.

Given the facts of culture and early socialization, defense against sexual harassment frequently falls to the *personality* of the particular woman or man. This is a slippery slope. It is dangerous to rely on an employee's *personal* history to stop sexual harassment.

Many psychologically normal and healthy women do not have good defenses against aggressive men. Correspondingly, men are socialized into gender roles that encourage the expression of aggression, but *not* in relation to women. If a woman harasses a man, he is as unprepared and vulnerable as is his harassed woman counterpart.

In each instance, early socialization clashes with present circumstance, and it falls to the *personality* strength of the individual to defend himself or herself.

This is why we need a law.

The effects of *socialization* and *personality* often contradict the social ideal of gender equity.

THE PRESCRIPTION

Laws change faster than people do.

If we need a law to prohibit sexual harassment as a form of discrimination based on gender, what does it take *psychologically* to enforce it in the workplace? To find an answer to this question, we need to learn more about how employees react to aggression, which is at the root of sexual harassment behavior.

We asked observers to watch five brief video vignettes of Richard interacting aggressively with the three coworkers you have encountered: Crystal, Liz, and Joe. Richard's aggression toward all three is superficially similar but, because of particular aspects of the situation, his hostility to Crystal and Liz may also be potentially "sexually harassing."

Beyond what they saw on video, the observers were given no information about any of the characters. They were then asked to rate how much they "*like*" Richard and how often they "*feel like*" Richard.

When we *like* a person, it is generally because we value qualities in that person. When we *feel like* a person, we see ourselves as similar or we identify with qualities in that person. As psychologists, we know that the relationship between how much we like or value someone and how much we can identify with him or her is one way to predict our capacity for empathy with that person.

Now we all agree that Richard has shown himself to be a rather disagreeable fellow in the interactions we have presented. Accordingly, we do not expect the observers to *like* Richard very much. And even if they secretly did, social desirability factors alone would prohibit them from admitting it!

Ask yourself this: Do you *like* Richard? Do you sometimes *feel like* Richard?

What do you think the observers reported?

Not unexpectedly, they *all* reported rather low rates of *liking* Richard. There is no surprise in that.

However, the *men* in the group reported *feeling like* Richard *more* than *liking* Richard. This means that although they recognized that his behavior was "wrong," they identified with his aggression. They could "put themselves in Richard's shoes."

In contrast, the women reported *feeling like* Richard *less* than *liking* him. This means that they too recognized his behavior as "wrong" but they did *not* identify with his aggression. They could not "put themselves in Richard's shoes."

The men and women did not respond in the same way to Richard's aggression. This has implications for training and reeducation. We need to find a vehicle that helps *all* employees divert a harassment outcome, understanding that there are individual differences in how people perceive and identify with aggression. These differences determine what strengths to build to promote self-protection.

Training that enhances empathy is an ideal method to help *both* genders prevent sexual harassment. Empathy is the process that allows us to "know" others by understanding them through *their* eyes, not only through our own. It is the psychological process that naturally inhibits aggression. Too often, our capacity to be empathic is limited by bringing only our own interpretations into play, forgetting that others may see the same situation quite differently. When this happens, we see only part of the picture and are less able to advocate for ourselves or be of help to others.

As we will see throughout this drama, empathy is a complex process, and it can derail for any one of a number of reasons. When it fails, we are stopped from building internal protections and mechanisms to cope effectively with workplace aggression.

This can happen to any party involved in a sexual harassment episode, man or woman, accuser, accused, coworker, manager, or executive officer. When riding in "the speedboat" of sexual harassment, we form critical judgments in a moment's time, often without full awareness of all aspects of the situation.

We need to "slow the speedboat down" in order to gain *empathic understanding* of the whole harassment situation. When we do, we are able to accurately interpret how the harasser intends the suspect behavior, how the victim or we feel about the situation, and what our procedural obligation is to take action. This is the armor we need to anticipate outcomes and respond proactively in determining the ultimate direction the sexual harassment "speedboat" will take.

Seeing the problem of Richard's hostile behavior in this broader light, it is reasonable to ask whether the prevention of sexual harassment should only fall on the shoulders of the target, who may often be *least* able to stop it for reasons of socialization and personality. Or, could enhancing the empathy of others in the organization also be of help?

Whose problem is sexual harassment, anyway?

Taking an example from our drama, we return to the "Welcome aboard" discussion between Richard and Joe. Richard is once again behaving badly. Business is not going well and, to make matters worse, Liz scores a success with Redman where Richard fails.

Richard's anxieties are triggered. So much so, in fact, that he is subconsciously thrown back to childhood memories, when he felt humiliated by a stern father who also made him feel inadequate.

Richard is not explicitly aware of all of this, but he nonetheless brings these experiences to work with him.

Richard drags his flagging self-esteem to the office of unsuspecting Joe. Gaining the admiration of others is Richard's antidote to feeling inadequate. You saw him do this before in his "snow job" of Griggs, as Liz so elegantly put it. Richard manipulated his boss into *praising* him when he had actually feared his boss's *recrimination* for not gaining security on the Redman account. Turning things around in this way is one of Richard's personality dynamics, and it is also one source of his hostile behavior.

Seeing Joe's door open, Richard mistakenly surmises that relief for his flagging self-esteem is on the way! He pops in on this young, less experienced manager—whom Richard sees as a potential source of comfort.

You may be saying to yourself that Richard is going about getting praise in all the wrong ways. His tactic to get Joe's admiration backfires. Why?

Joe does not perceive Richard as wanting his approval! He is blindsided by his own ambition. Joe reacts to Richard from the perspective of *his* self-interest. He wonders who this Richard really is, and whether an alliance with him serves *Joe's* career interest.

This orientation prevents Joe from establishing empathy for Richard, whom he correctly perceives as an aggressive "tiger in a cage." Returning aggression with aggression, as *his* socialization experiences have taught him, Joe goes head-to-head with the tiger. Richard leaves as angry, as dissatisfied, and as *hungry* for validation as when he walked in!

Richard is en route to Denny's Pub to have lunch with Crystal. Would *you* want to be his "lady in waiting" right around now?

Joe, Liz, and Crystal do nothing to curb Richard's hostility. If any one of them had had a more empathic understanding of Richard, the harassment outcome might have been quite different.

We need to learn more about empathy and how it works to inhibit aggression.

CHAPTER FOUR

Speak Now or You'll Forever Have No Peace

You will explore the next condition of quid pro quo sexual harassment that sexual advances of the supervisor are unwelcome. This is sometimes hard to determine, based only on the surface interactions between the harassment partners. When either party's intention is left open to interpretation, the waters get muddied and distortions form. It can then be difficult to apply this seemingly unambiguous legal standard.

$\mathcal{R}$ichard's harassment of Crystal has escalated unchecked during her first six months of employment as his administrative assistant in the American Corporation. Now in full tilt, Richard makes propositions, engages in heavily provocative innuendo, and touches Crystal to communicate his pleasure in being near her. She has picked up some steam in her struggle to fend off his advances, but her protest is too little and too late to deter Richard.

Richard knows exactly how to play this young administrative assistant to his best advantage. If Crystal succumbs and does not declare to her harasser that his conduct is unwelcome, does her submission imply consent?

THE SCENE

Richard sauntered into Denny's Pub and sidled into the booth that he usually reserved when dining with his "special" friend. Crystal had not yet arrived. Richard looked at his watch and sighed—1:05 P.M. She was already *five* minutes late!

Richard removed some papers from his attaché and spread them out carefully on the table in front of him. A travel log, a restaurant guide, and some printed information on securing a booth in the convention center. Richard had an important agenda. He straightened his tie and made ready to present his proposal to Crystal for the trade show in Las Vegas.

The waiter came up to Richard. "Are you ready to order, sir?"

"No!" The waiter disappeared.

Richard glanced again at his watch. With growing discomfort, he rearranged the travel papers — his props. He pretended to pore over the details of the itinerary so that when Crystal arrived he would appear to be absorbed in his convention planning and not mired in the personal insecurity that was triggered by her tardiness.

"*Ten* minutes late!" Richard's discomfort mounted to irritation.

The waiter again made his appearance, though this time he had the wisdom to be silent.

"No, no, not yet." Richard muttered in reply, as though the waiter had spoken to him. He formally dismissed him with a wave of the hand.

As the waiter turned to go, Richard had a second thought. "Wait! I'll have a scotch on the rocks. Make it a double."

Richard looked anxiously at his watch once more. "*Fifteen* minutes late!"

A blush of embarrassment reddened Richard's face. He could barely contain the disturbing thought that perhaps Crystal had decided not to come.

The waiter served Richard his double scotch.

The burning liquor soothed Richard's scratchy throat. His thoughts drifted away from Crystal. He now noticed the couples in the adjacent booths and wondered if he was being regarded with pity, being obviously alone. Or, worse yet, how would he explain himself if someone from the corporation wandered in and found him without a partner, dining alone in this obvious *twosome* accommodation?

This train of thought was as disturbing as the possibility of Crystal's deserting him. But Richard was still unwilling to openly consider that perhaps Crystal did not intend to keep her lunch date with him.

Richard's glass was empty. The scotch had taken its good effect. He was relaxed; the tension was drained from his body.

One twenty-five!

"Time stands still for no one!" Richard snapped his fingers to get the waiter's attention.

A consummate professional, the waiter understood Richard's gesture to mean that he had best remove the second place setting from opposite this guest, in order to not call attention to the now apparent fact that he had been stood up.

Richard ordered lunch.

Crystal mentally checked off each street sign she passed as she hurried north to get back to work before her lunch hour was up. She had chosen a coffee shop as far away from American as possible, while still allowing herself enough time to get back to her desk before 2:00 P.M.

The cold wind tore through her thin jacket. The distance she had traveled seemed longer now that she was going back to work. Crystal knew that the difference in perception was a direct result of the dread she felt in the pit of her stomach.

Mr. Whatman had again asked her to go to lunch with him at Denny's Pub. Crystal was not going to fall for the trap this time, though—no matter what. The first time he had asked her to meet him for lunch, she thought the purpose was to discuss business.

"And discuss business Richard did. *Monkey* business!"

Crystal recalled with no small measure of shame and embarrassment that she had agreed to go the second time because she couldn't think of an acceptable excuse quickly enough.

"Coward!" Crystal admonished herself for past weakness even as she tried to forgive herself her flaws. Today was trial three. In a move of rare defiance, Crystal simply did not show up for Mr. Whatman's private luncheon.

"Perhaps he will take the hint," prayed a beleaguered Crystal.

Crystal entered the American Corporation and pressed the elevator button to summon the car that would take her up to her cubicle on the twenty-fourth floor. For a fleeting moment, she had a fantasy that Mr. Whatman would not return to the office that afternoon.

She had no such luck.

"Ah, Crystal, you are back from lunch. I thought you would be at Denny's Pub. I was looking for you."

Richard tried to sound casual as he leaned over Crystal, who was seated at her workstation.

When Crystal did not reply, Richard added defensively, "Of course, *strictly business!*"

Crystal knew that she could not ignore Mr. Whatman. He would persist until she answered him. She forced herself to rise above her intimidation and handle her problem with Richard professionally.

"Mr. Whatman, I *told* you that I was not going to meet there anymore. How can I help you now?"

Richard was feeling pretty mellow in spite of Crystal's resistance; the alcohol was boosting his confidence. His hands found their way to her shoulders. Massaging her rhythmically, he replied, "You are helping me already! And call me *Richie!*"

"How could this be happening to me *again*," groaned a panicked Crystal under her breath. She swiveled abruptly in her seat in an attempt to wrest herself free of Richard's grip. His hands fell from her shoulders and a look of what seemed to Crystal to be annoyance crossed his face.

Fast losing ground, Crystal stammered, "I mean, what do you *want?*"

Score one for Richard. She was succumbing to his charm. Let the games begin!

"What are you giving away?" he asked seductively. Richard triumphantly reclaimed Crystal's shoulders in his hands.

She was all too familiar with Richard's next move. He would badger her, playing on her words, until his fun was through.

"What I mean, Mr. Whatman, is *why are you here now?*"

Crystal overarticulated each syllable, as if this were the source of Richard's confusion in understanding her. For added emphasis, she again swiveled around in her chair to loosen Richard's grip, this time upping the ante by shooting a direct and disapproving gaze at him.

Score two for Richard. Crystal was catching on nicely to his playful repartee. She was fighting back.

"Why am I *here?*" Richard thoroughly enjoyed this sport. "Why are *any* of us here, Crystal?"

She did not know what to say.

Just then, Joe came into view in the hallway, in their mutual line of vision. Crystal was not certain how long Joe had been there, or whether he had noticed that Mr. Whatman had been massaging her shoulders only moments earlier. Instinctively, Richard straightened up and put his hands in his pockets as Joe passed the cubicle.

Both Crystal and Richard simultaneously smiled a greeting to Joe.

"Good girl," thought Richard. "Crystal kept up her end."

"Damn it," thought Crystal. "I don't think Joe saw anything."

"Yes, Crystal, you are really working out well in this office."

Richard brushed his hand across Crystal's face, gently placing her long hair to one side. He was comforted to know that he and his Crystal were safe in their shared private universe.

THE DIAGNOSIS

This scene opens up discussion on the second condition of quid pro quo harassment: Sexual advances are *unwelcome*. If a subordinate submits to a supervisor's advance out of fear of reprisal or retaliation, it may still be considered *unwelcome*. An element of coercion is implicit in the case of supervisor sexual harassment. Submission does not necessarily imply consent.

It may seem obvious to you when a sexual advance is *unwelcome*, but Crystal has a bear of a struggle in this scene.

The harassment contract has taken shape over the past six months, and expectations have been set—and met, apparently—during this time frame. In Richard's mind, he and Crystal are in agreement about the terms and conditions of their coupling, and he has no inkling that she is in any conflict regarding their mutual liaison.

Crystal, on the contrary, "wants out" of the deal. But unable (or perhaps unwilling) to get out during the early engagement period, she unwittingly allowed Richard to believe that she is in agreement with his advances.

This is not an unusual set of circumstances in quid pro quo sexual harassment.

It is easy to dismiss this harassment couple's problem as a simple case of "He is in denial" and "She is too intimidated to tell him *No.*" Then we can drop all other concerns, "blame" Richard, and move on. Case closed!

But have we gone far enough in our analysis? Legally, perhaps we have. Liability is absolute when the supervisor issues unwelcome sexual advances to a subordinate in exchange for favorable work conditions. Psychologically, however, the picture is not as clear.

Let's see what happens if we analyze this harassment couple a little more closely.

Yes, Crystal is intimidated. Her response to Richard's hostility and "bully" tactics is appeasement. Unable to cope effectively with aggression, Crystal accommodates. This is a response she learned early in life. We can assume that, in Crystal's past, deferring to authority was expected, "polite," or even rewarded.

Accordingly, we may also assume that, in the beginning, Crystal does not anticipate that her appeasement of Richard will lead her into trouble.

Now ask yourself: Did Crystal consent to Richard's advances in the beginning of the engagement period? What if she did not realize that she was heading into harassment? How should we conceive of *consent* in this context?

And thus far, whose *fault* is it?

Let's continue. Crystal becomes aware at some point during the first six months that appeasing Richard does not satisfy him. Accommodation only encourages Richard in his path of seduction. What she has learned early in life does not serve her well now.

Crystal goes into a panic. She knows that she is in hot water because she must now make a shift and approach Mr. Whatman from another direction if she is to extricate herself from the trap she finds herself in. Crystal feels ashamed of herself and angry with her boss for placing her in this situation. You may blame only Richard, but Crystal also blames herself.

This is where we find Crystal now. She is anxiously trying a second tactic to get out of a bad situation. With little or no life experience to inform her on what might work, Crystal goes into reverse. If appeasement does not work, maybe refusal will.

Ask again: By refusing to share lunch with Mr. Whatman, is Crystal "standing up to" the harassment and saying *No?*

We would have to say *No* to each possibility. Crystal is still struggling with her *relationship* to Mr. Whatman, and she is not emotionally separate enough to treat his hostility as behavior that "does not belong to her." She still feels, deep down, that she is a part of what is transpiring between them. She is still part of a couple emotionally.

Crystal asks Richard's permission to excuse her from the harassment table. But Richard chooses not to hear Crystal's request.

His reaction to Crystal is evidence enough that he is misinterpreting Crystal's behavior as just another phase in their liaison. He does not know precisely what she is trying to communicate by failing to keep the lunch date, but he does not perceive her as trying to "get out." He thinks they are playing a game of cat and mouse.

Richard wants things to go on with Crystal, and his judgment is clouded by his misperception. Is this a crime?

Crystal, meanwhile, *thinks* that her communication is clear as water to Mr. Whatman. After all, it took all her courage to *not* go to Denny's Pub after being summoned there by her boss. How could he not know? But reread her dialogue to Mr. Whatman. Has Crystal been as clear as she thinks?

The law says that, in quid pro quo sexual harassment, *unwelcome* sexual advances have occurred.

Has that happened here?

This sexual harassment contract is near a breaking point. Crystal's feelings of helplessness and entrapment are intensifying. If she is like most quid pro quo "victims," she will redouble her efforts to get away from Mr. Whatman.

However, her one critical distortion—that Richard *knows* she wants out and is therefore *refusing* to respect her boundaries—could cost her dearly if it persists uncorrected.

Crystal and Richard are approaching a psychological cornerstone. What happens next will predict the final outcome of this corporate "thriller." Richard does *not* know what Crystal *thinks* she is communicating to him. *She* does not know that *he* does not know.

Richard thinks Crystal is playing along with him, side by side, enjoying the "sport" they play so well together. Richard likes "my Crystal," as he refers to her.

Crystal is about ready to crack.

When Richard finally notices Crystal's "change of heart," what emotions do you imagine will be engendered?

Now imagine these two in a court of law a few years down the road, recalling to a jury the events of this time period. Crystal asserts her perception that she *tried* to tell her boss *No*, but he wouldn't listen. She *believed* her job depended on her submission to his requests.

Is Crystal lying?

Richard defends himself by saying that he may be accused of exercising poor judgment in conducting a romantic relationship with his subordinate, but he did not *harass* her. Crystal *wanted* to meet him.

Is Richard lying?

We repeat, the law says that, in quid pro quo sexual harassment, *unwelcome* sexual advances have occurred. Psychologically, does this capture what has transpired between Richard and Crystal? Or is the matter more ambiguous?

THE PRESCRIPTION

The decision about whether sexual advances are welcome proves to be complicated in many instances of supervisor sexual harassment. The legal stand on coercion is unambiguous.

But when the psychodynamics of the actual harassment couple are factored into the legal equation, the boundary between consent and refusal is always blurred.

You may argue that it is best to avoid any possibility of confusion and follow the ironclad rule that supervisors may *never* date subordinates. Some companies have put this prohibition into effect in the hope of putting an end, once and for all, to any possibility of supervisor sexual harassment.

But it is awfully hard to enforce even ironclad rules about human behavior. The statistics on dating in the workplace would corroborate this fact. Recent surveys on this issue report that up to 80 percent of all workers know of, or have been involved in, office romances; and approximately one-third of all dating relationships start at work.

Yet, when we present this tale of Crystal and Richard in our sexual harassment training sessions, employees demand "rules!"

Tell us what to do!

People *want* to see Richard's harassment of Crystal in black and white. They *want* to lay blame so that they can gain closure on the discomforting emotions that the harassment stirs up. They have studied the definition of quid pro quo sexual harassment and *want* to apply a set of logical or legal rules to identify a culprit.

Then they would not have to acknowledge their emotions.

But here is a baffling finding. Amid this frantic scurrying for rules, when we measure the *emotional* responses of observers in our lab to Crystal and Richard in this scene, a very different picture emerges.

What would you expect?

In the training room, desperate to close the case, employees usually blame Richard because "He is the boss [and] should know better." We therefore predicted that the observers would correspondingly have *increased* empathy for Crystal, the helpless "victim" of Richard's harassment.

We were wrong.

Crystal receives her lowest ratings on the *Like* scale and still lower ratings on the *Feel Like* scale for the episode you just read. Our subjects have little empathy for Crystal. They have all but given up on her.

What is going on? We are witnessing a split between how people think about whether Crystal consented and how they feel about it. They are outwardly defending Crystal and blaming Richard, but inwardly they are angry with Crystal!

Upon reflection, however, this paradox makes sense. The responses are an experimental model of "blaming the victim." Unable to "get right" with the conflicted emotions the sexual harassment evokes, the observers blame the object that causes the upset.

If Crystal were stronger, this whole mess wouldn't have happened at all!

So far, all of these reactions and conflicts are hidden from awareness because the sexual harassment has not yet risen to the surface in the corporation. It is only going on inside the characters you have met—the harasser, the victim, and the coworkers.

But take stock. You will revisit *all* of these conflicts again, if and when the sexual harassment is disclosed, and in a more virulent form than ever. It is important to note now that employee emotions about the sexual harassment have been brewing internally for a long time. Distortion compounds distortion as "fact" clashes with "affect."

Many of these contradictions fall below the threshold of awareness and are therefore not accessible to the people who are experiencing them. But they are nevertheless profoundly influencing their behavior and shaping the sexual harassment outcome.

CHAPTER FIVE

Sexual Harassment Is
Subtle to Whom?

You will explore the next condition of hostile environment sexual harassment that unwelcome behavior is severe or pervasive. Most instances of this form of harassment fall in a "subtle" but pervasive category. The recipient of subtle harassment often perceives the large intentions that hide behind even small acts of hostility. By focusing only on hostile acts, we run the risk of ignoring the serious problems that cause them.

T *he scene begins with Liz cheerfully closing her quarter's-end accounts. Things are looking up for her since the Redman break-through. After many unsuccessful attempts, alone and with Richard, to engage this difficult client using traditional meth-ods, Liz designed a clever plan. Redman signed off on the cre-ative proposal, scoring a professional victory for Liz and a profitable outcome for both corporations.*

Richard is not elated. Liz's victory is his defeat. Richard is not opposed to the Redman Plan but is irritated that he didn't think of it first. The tables have turned; Richard is no longer "on top." The two managers are having a business meeting. Richard is jealous of Liz, who is more confident than ever before. The ground is now fertile for a hostile exchange.

THE SCENE

Liz was humming softly to herself as she added up the columns on the far side of the ledger. She felt proud, better than she had felt in a long time. The Redman Plan was a hit. For months, Liz and Richard had been struggling unsuccess-fully to plot a strategy that would convince this client to come on board. Traditional wisdom had fallen by the wayside, not because it was wrong, but because Redman had too many fa-vorites and loyalty ties to other entities. American just wasn't top on their list.

Richard was no help, either. He kept doing end runs around Liz. She noticed, early in the negotiations, that although she would freely share critical information with him, he would keep all of his insights and discoveries to himself.

Liz pulled away from Richard after the meeting with Griggs, when Richard grandstanded his achievements to the CEO at her expense. She determined that she would have to solve her problems with Redman herself. Richard could not be trusted.

Liz was surprised to find that Richard didn't mind a bit when she withdrew. He did not seem to care that she communicated less and less to him about her progress with Redman. She quietly set about the task of designing a new solution to the problem.

Time passed in seeming slow motion, and desperation gave way to despondency. Liz had to come to terms with the possibility that this might be an account that she could not hope to win. Nowhere is it required that *every* contract be satisfied, but Redman was a "political hot potato," and losing the bid unfortunately carried strong negative consequences.

Finally, a breakthrough came to Liz. She had not even been thinking about Redman, but in designing a portfolio for another company, she got a really wild idea. With nothing to lose, she put together a clever proposal. She played around with all of the possibilities she could think of. The plan worked.

No one was more surprised than Richard when Liz presented the unconventional Redman Plan to him on the telephone that day. She had not bothered to run the plan past Richard first. She had taken her idea directly to Griggs.

Richard was mad. The thought did cross his mind, however, that part of his annoyance may have been because Liz had masterminded the plan.

Liz, not Richard, would get credit for the contract.

Richard knocked on Liz's door. "Can I come in?"

Liz was absorbed in her work. Looking up, she saw Richard already halfway across her room.

"Why doesn't he ever *wait* to be invited in?" she thought with irritation.

Concealing her emotions, Liz replied with a half-hearted wave of her hand, heralding Richard in.

"So," thought Richard, "now that she won Redman, she thinks she is top dog!"

Richard stood opposite Liz, across the desk, eyeing the empty chair at her side. Why didn't Liz offer him the seat? Richard took offense inwardly at this slight. Perhaps she thought them equals, now that Griggs was in her back pocket.

"I'm about to close out the quarter on the Redman account and want to go over the final figures with you. You worked on this account, too," Richard said blandly.

Liz bristled at Richard's statement that she had "worked on this account, too." She answered his comment silently to herself. "No, Richard, I didn't *work on* this account, I *won* this account!"

Liz held back her comment, not wanting to get into a battle of wills with Richard. She was still on his team for the Redman deal, and they had to coordinate their results in order to give Griggs one report. Liz indicated the empty chair next to her desk.

"Sit down, Richard."

Richard moved his chair closer to Liz as he placed the folder on the desk for Liz to inspect. She did not respond immediately.

Impatient, Richard quipped, "How's about you look over *here?*" and he pointed to the folder.

Liz leaned in to examine Richard's dossier. Richard leaned in too, maybe a tad more than was absolutely necessary for the purpose at hand. Liz scanned the figures.

Richard scanned Liz.

"Hm, you smell good. New shampoo you're using?" Richard was trying to be friendly.

Liz opted for the path of least resistance. She made no reply to Richard's remark but shot him a menacing glance.

"These figures look right to me." Liz pushed the folder away, wishing she could push Richard away as well. "They're the ones I entered last week. Anything else you want me to see?"

Richard reacted negatively to Liz. She was giving him short shrift. He could not fathom why, but he sensed that she did not care to labor over this discussion with him any longer than was necessary.

Richard felt uneasy. He was not content to leave things as they were. He felt Liz was not being very respectful toward him.

"But why not?" he thought in a flash of anger. "Does she no longer value what I contributed to the team, now that Griggs approved her Redman Plan?"

"My, my, aren't we moody today," Richard commented. "Is it *that* time of the month?"

Richard knew he was being testy. But Liz started it.

The path of least resistance was a flop. Without much thought, Liz stepped up to the plate.

"Really, Richard, why don't you give it up? I have told you before that I don't appreciate your remarks."

"Who can understand these women?" thought Richard.

Yet he somehow felt reassured. At least Liz was paying attention to him. Anything was better than her arrogant dismissal.

Their business concluded, Richard made ready to leave. He had a busy schedule, and his composure was impeccable. With exaggerated officiousness, Richard returned the chair in which he had been sitting to the exact spot from whence it came.

"*Some* people just have no sense of humor. You know, Liz, you really oughta lighten up. You are just *too serious!*"

THE DIAGNOSIS

The next condition of hostile environment sexual harassment is that the unwelcome behavior is *severe* or *pervasive*. The Supreme Court included both criteria because it recognized that a single act may be severe enough to create a hostile environment, or successive acts—none of which, alone, is of sufficient magnitude—can cumulatively interfere with working conditions. Richard's behavior toward Liz borders on the *pervasive* criterion, based on the information we have been given.

Is there an important difference, other than in magnitude, between the two types of hostile environment acts—those that are severe and those that are pervasive? Interestingly, the *less severe* an act is in magnitude, the *greater its frequency* of actual occurrence in the workplace.

Let us explore this inverse relationship between the severity of an act and the frequency of its occurrence. *Severe* acts, though less common, are more easily recognized as *hostile* acts. Their aggressive nature is obvious.

Pervasive acts, though often of a lesser magnitude of severity, are more difficult to identify. Hence the currently popular term "subtle" sexual harassment. Subtle acts often take the form of verbal comments, visual gazes and leers, off-color jokes, and offensive visual displays.

The most intriguing question about this class of pervasive but not severe acts is: To whom are they subtle?

Certainly no employee who has been the butt of this kind of behavior finds it *subtle* in the least. Even schoolchildren are sensitive to subtle teasing on the playground and will accurately identify it as "not in good fun."

Adults in the workplace are at least as savvy as schoolchildren at recognizing subtle hostility. The hostility of an act resides not only in its overt form of expression but also in the intentions of the actor.

Most of us do not need to be bopped over the head to know when we are the target of aggression. We perceive aggression according to both the intentions of the actor and the intensity of the act committed.

So again we ask: To whom is subtle sexual harassment subtle? If not to the victim, then to whom?

The answer is: Subtle sexual harassment is subtle only to the harasser. The hostility that is communicated in these instances is most often below the radar screen of the actor, not the recipient. And that which is not acknowledged is doomed to be repeated.

Because this is the most common form of workplace harassment, it is important to understand how hostile acts become pervasive acts, and why they are so hard to stop.

We can learn something about subtle but pervasive workplace hostility from looking below the surface of the scene between Richard and Liz. How were hostile intentions communicated?

Liz is offended when Richard intrudes into her office without invitation. She believes Richard violates her boundary in bypassing her permission to enter her private space. Liz assumes further that Richard knows the rules of social commerce and intentionally chooses to disregard common courtesy. She strikes back with the issuance of only a lukewarm greeting.

Richard feels rebuffed by Liz. Not aware of the source of her annoyance at him, he retaliates with a volley of return hostility. He insists that Liz pay better attention to his business concerns and pushes his folder in her face.

Richard and Liz are sparring, though neither yet acknowledges it to the other.

Richard is the more impatient of the two. His aggression rises to the surface first. He takes a verbal pot shot at Liz in the form of the "shampoo" remark.

Now war is declared. Liz returns Richard's volley. She tells him off!

The scene ends in a *hostility stalemate*. Both parties are angry and each thinks the other knows exactly why.

This sequence should be familiar to you. We saw something like it before, with Richard and Crystal. Liz, however, is not Richard's subordinate but his colleague. Accordingly, his verbal statements to Liz may be even more offensive on the surface than his verbal seductive innuendo to Crystal in the first scene, but the present exchange is an example of only subtle sexual harassment.

Given that distinction, you can begin to appreciate the difficulty in judging the *severity* of sexual harassment on the basis of the harassment *act*.

We decided to investigate the relationship between the harassment act and perception of the severity of an act.

We asked observers to compare Richard's *hostility* to Liz in the present exchange to the hostility shown to Crystal in the first and second scenes.

How do you think the observers judged Richard?

Objectively, only his "humor" toward Liz is offensive. But he *touches* Crystal, uses *seductive* language, and, in the first scene, he refers to her in terms that are *demeaning*.

The observers found Richard more aggressive in relation to Liz!

The perception of hostility is a ubiquitous thing. The most *subtle* of all hostile acts were rated as the most *aggressive*.

THE PRESCRIPTION

When they are presented with Richard's provocative behavior toward Liz, why do the employees we see in training get charged up far in excess of the actual acts committed? What are they reacting to?

Let's go back and examine the dialogue between Liz and Richard more carefully. At what level is Richard's assault of Liz most menacing?

What is most offensive and perhaps even threatening about Richard's hostility is actually left unnoticed by Liz. In her retorts to Richard, she focuses on his explicit verbal acts and exhorts him to stop saying those things. But is this really the heart of the matter?

Imagine Liz in a court of law. What would she say? "Your Honor, Richard said, 'You smell good,' and he asked me if it is *that* time of the month." Richard's harassment does not sound like much when it is reduced to a literal transcription of his words.

You will recall that we spoke of the difference between the *intention* behind the commission of a hostile act and the actual *act* undertaken. What hurts Liz the most, and is most damaging to their work relationship, is Richard's *intention* in making these offensive verbal remarks to her.

Richard's uncooperative and sneaky attitude, his lack of generosity in celebrating Liz's success, his incapacity to be a team player—and, finally, his unwillingness to acknowledge his problem and his displacement of his negative feelings onto Liz—are all foreboding.

Could it be that *all* this gets rolled into the perception of Richard's harassment acts?

And what does Liz respond to? Richard's *intentions* or his *words?* She reacts to his harassment language only, as if wiping Richard's words away will solve their workplace problem.

This suits Richard just fine. In fact, he invites it. Why?

Richard does not want to, or know how to, solve the workplace conflict that gave rise to his hostility. He too is stuck. He certainly knows that he is tense, upset, on the edge. He may even have some insight into why. But he cannot use that awareness.

Richard is threatened by the change in Liz and, more generally, by the pervasive changes in the global corporation. Unable to relieve his anxieties, he instead tries to ignore them. No use, for soon his anger and insecurity erupt, but in a disguised form. Richard's "joking" is his way of letting off steam. It transfers his hostility onto a seemingly "safe" target—Liz.

Liz, in turn, has been playing hide-and-seek with Richard's hostility for a long time. Not willing to express to him directly her disappointment for their failed collaboration on the Redman account, she has instead avoided him. Skirting the conflict, she has treated Richard as she feels he has treated her.

The *hostility stalemate* entraps both Richard and Liz. Each allows it to stop their communication. By focusing their joint attention on the red herring of Richard's harassing verbal acts, they divert their attention away from the more disturbing workplace conflict that lies beneath those acts.

This dynamic of displaced hostility is quite common in hostile environment harassment. And this is why it is so hard for employers and employees to put an end to it. The harassment incident is often only a screen for deeper workplace conflicts. The harassment acts themselves may seem mild or even "trifling" when reduced to concrete description—a look, a picture, a word, a stare, a joke—but the conflicts that underlie them can be enormous.

When symptoms and not problems are the focus of attention, solutions are not found. The interpersonal or organizational problem that gives rise to subtle sexual harassment will grow, recur, or resurface in new ways. Confronting the harassment on the surface will do little good to solve the problem.

Alternatively, if subtle coworker harassment acts are approached as indicators of serious workplace breaches, steps can be taken to remedy root causes. Had Richard and Liz addressed their subtle hostility in the exchanges that transpired over the Redman account, do you think the "shampoo" remark would have been the focus of their attention?

CHAPTER SIX

His *Quid* for Her *Quo*

You will explore the next condition for quid pro quo sexual harassment that sexual favors are demanded in exchange for favorable work conditions. This is the essence of supervisor harassment, when differences in authority are abused for personal gain. The law can correct for the tangible inequities created by a quid pro quo sexual harasser, but it is left to the corporation to correct for the psychological inequities. These are more ambiguous and, if ignored, potentially threatening.

*L*iz *suspects that Richard upsets other women in the office, but she has no idea that Crystal is suffering in silence and is alone in her struggle. Crystal is fighting a losing battle. She finally succeeds in rebuffing Richard's sexual advances, but her trouble does not stop here. Crystal's office communication with Mr. Whatman deteriorates, and her work regresses as a result of the harassment strain. Crystal is convinced that there is nothing left to save.*

Richard recognizes the change in Crystal but does not know its cause. He is disillusioned with her. Crystal is a disappointment. Richard notices her lack of spunk and enthusiasm, and he accepts with resignation that she does not want to form a close working relationship with him. He had hoped for a better outcome with this fading starlet.

One year after her employment began, Richard is giving Crystal her annual performance review. He informs her of his concern regarding her slacking performance, and he gives the harassed Crystal a negative performance appraisal. The first line of defense—for Richard and Crystal—has failed to prevent sexual harassment.

THE SCENE

Crystal's head was throbbing. A change had come over her after she left Mr. Whatman sitting alone in Denny's Pub. That was six months ago. Crystal shuddered at the memory of that day, the panic she had felt walking up and down the avenue in the freezing cold trying to talk sense into herself so that she would not buckle under the pressure to spend another lunch hour with her seductive boss. She could not take it anymore. Crystal vowed to free herself once and for all from Mr. Whatman's grip.

Back then, Crystal thought that confronting Mr. Whatman would be enough to correct the problem. She imagined that her boss would eventually respect her for standing up to him, even if he was a little annoyed at first by her refusal. He would get used to it. No longer a prisoner to intimidation, Crystal would be strong and steady, not wobbly and humiliated as she was when she caved in to his bullying.

The illogic of this line of thinking was glaring to Crystal now. Not only did Mr. Whatman *not* respect her more for standing up to him, but their communication in the office took a turn for the worse. When they both returned from their separate lunches that day, Mr. Whatman let her know, in no uncertain terms, that he was displeased with her. Leaning over her desk, he invaded her personal space, demanding that she explain her absence from the pub luncheon. He was very pushy and aggressive. He denied her the satisfaction of acknowledging her refusal as a sign of strength. Caught off guard, she again let him walk all over her.

But that was the last time. Something got triggered within Crystal, and it pushed her over a critical threshold she did not know she had. With quiet but steely persistence, over the next few weeks, she gradually pushed back against Mr. Whatman's every advance. He seemed surprised at first, but finally stopped approaching her in that creepy way. Correction: He stopped approaching her at all, except to deliver criticism or make a snide remark. Crystal spent most workdays feeling that Mr. Whatman thought she could do nothing right.

Crystal had misgivings. When Mr. Whatman was after her in a seductive way, he was also nice to her. She was very aware that he treated her differently from the other women in the office. Crystal was embarrassed by this because she knew it was "wrong" to enjoy this special treatment on the one hand and then reject his advances on the other. After she turned him away, she was relieved of the burden of this discomfort. However, her reward for doing the right thing was equal (mis)treatment with others in Mr. Whatman's division.

Tallying up the final score, Crystal realized that she had gained NOTHING in rebuking Mr. Whatman, and had in fact *lost* a great deal. He afforded her no greater respect in the office. She felt no better about herself outside the office. Mr. Whatman complained about her every mistake, often in front of other people. Her dread in facing him grew stronger by the day. Throughout this ordeal, her attention to her work had diminished. Her concentration was shot. She did not know how to regain Mr. Whatman's trust. In all, Crystal hated getting up in the morning and coming to work.

It was one year to the day after her employment began at American, and Mr. Whatman was scheduled to deliver to Crystal her annual performance review. Judgment Day. Crystal did not know what to expect. She felt as though she was standing on gelatin.

Crystal had reason to worry.

Richard had come to accept the change in Crystal. He had seen this pattern before, in some of his other young administrative assistants. Fresh out of school, they came to work ready to set the world ablaze. They burned out just as quickly. Crystal was only another passing comet, a disappointment.

Richard didn't blame himself. He had tried to get close to Crystal. He had shared in her high expectations when she first came on board at American, and he offered her many opportunities to "do extra" and build a career for herself in the corporation. His behavior had been above reproach.

Could he be so bad a judge of character, Richard wondered? What went wrong?

Richard did not know the answer to this question, though he had to accept that Crystal's star had all but burned to extinction. And things between them had soured. Richard would not ordinarily dwell too long or worry about losing an assistant, but something else about the Crystal situation made him decidedly uncomfortable.

Richard didn't trust the "new" Crystal. She had a most unanticipated change of heart toward him and her job. When she began her employment in American, she was enthusiastic about work and enjoyed their joking around as much as he. She could have gone far in the company.

About their personal affairs, Crystal was free to draw the line anywhere she wanted to. Instead of taking advantage of her opportunities with him, Crystal gave him a crossed directional. For a while, the light was green. Naturally, Richard proceeded. But then Crystal changed her mind and turned the light red, for no apparent reason. Richard hadn't done anything different.

He was irritated. Crystal had him in a headlock, and Richard knew it. He could easily forgive Crystal her fickleness because she was immature and not terribly important to him in the first place. She was just another stop along the highway. But she had turned the tables on him, and Richard could not afford to be vulnerable to her whim. He had to find a way to protect himself from any potential harm Crystal could bring down around him.

Richard wondered: Was Crystal really so innocent? An alternative explanation for Crystal's apparent change of heart nagged at Richard. "Maybe she is more of a menace than I suspected," Richard worried. Perhaps he had badly misjudged Crystal's character and she was not so naïve after all.

Could Richard have been blindsided?

Richard reassured himself with thoughts that Crystal could not get even with him even if this was her intention. She worked only in Richard's division, and no one other than his direct reports had access to her. He was convinced that if the situation came down to her word against his, no one would believe Crystal even if she did talk. And as far as Griggs was concerned, Richard was worth a lot more to the company than Crystal was. Richard banked on the importance of the bottom line to shield him from Crystal's line of fire.

This was all true, but Richard was still troubled. He knew that a perception of foul play could be nearly as damaging to his credibility as Crystal's exposition of her "truth" about what had happened.

Richard had to do something to protect himself and keep this molehill from becoming a mountain. He had to play an offensive game. Richard skillfully tooled his performance appraisal of Crystal. It had to include the ammunition he *might* need to have on record if he was forced to build a defense for

himself against her attempted character assassination, but not
be obviously biased or blatantly untruthful, lest she scream
back "Discrimination!"

It was time to put Crystal in checkmate.

"Crystal, you and I need to talk." Richard invited Crystal
to sit down. It was time for her annual review.

Crystal took her usual seat, opposite her boss. She was
nervous because her intuition told her that this was not going
to be an easy meeting. Would she have the courage to speak
out if Mr. Whatman gave her a bad evaluation?

"You have been slipping, lately. I wanted to give you a better review, but in all good conscience, your work of late has
simply *not* justified it."

At the close of this remark, Crystal realized that her intuition was correct. Mr. Whatman was going to roast her over the
coals. He handed her a printed form that had check marks and
comments written across it. Crystal read the document.

"And I don't have to tell you, unless you earn more points,
your raise will not be the one I know you hoped for." Richard
admonished Crystal with a stern and punishing stare, caution-
ing her against arguing back.

This was Crystal's opportunity. She knew that if she caved
in now, she would be handing the reins over to Mr. Whatman
without so much as a whimper. It almost didn't matter what
she said, but she had to let him know that she saw what he was
up to.

"With all due respect, sir, I do not understand why you
rated me as you did." Scanning the document, she continued,

"Here, you wrote '*Needs improvement*' in the category '*Takes initiative.*' Really? What *else* should I have done?"

Crystal had a bewildered look. For a moment, Richard almost felt sorry for her. She was an easy prey, and he didn't really want to hurt her. But then he reminded himself that she could change the traffic light from green to red in a heartbeat. Feeling sorry for her was a trap, and he must think only about protecting himself.

"Now, Crystal. You can be such a stubborn child! Didn't I invite you to attend the convention as my personal assistant?" Richard glowered at Crystal, who shrank at his angry tone, reminding her of this event.

"Didn't I?" Richard's volume was rising, and Crystal could feel her intimidation show in her gentle shuddering. She hated it when this happened. She felt that her weakness was transparent to her accuser.

She nodded *yes*. "And did you go? Did you take advantage of *that* opportunity to better yourself? No, no. You have definitely been backing off, wouldn't you say?"

It was a new sensation, but Crystal could *feel* her intimidation turn to anger at Mr. Whatman. Determination overtook fear. She had made a promise to herself not to "go blank," as the "old" Crystal would have done.

"You and I both know why," Crystal replied in a quiet but steely whisper.

With his impatience growing, Richard felt compelled to end this unpleasant meeting. "Well, Crystal, it is up to you. You know what you need to improve on if you wish to get ahead here. The choice is all yours." And Crystal was dismissed.

THE DIAGNOSIS

The next condition of supervisor sexual harassment is that sexual favors are demanded in exchange for favorable treatment or continued employment. Quid pro quo sexual harassment occurs when an employer attempts to make an employee *submit to sexual demands as a condition of his or her employment.* Refusal by the employee may be conditioned to threatened or actual retaliation by the employer, in the form of loss of tangible benefits or denial of future opportunities. Termination from the job, unfavorable performance review, pass-over for promotion, or loss of salary are among the more common reprisals threatened by harassing employers.

As already noted, quid pro quo means literally *this for that.* Richard delivered the "quo" to Crystal for refusing his "quid." The judgment he reached, about her prospects to advance in the company, was based (at least in part) on her refusal to engage in certain activities with him. Prior to this exchange, his interactions with her might have been construed as in a "gray zone" from a strictly legal perspective, although we have not seen enough to make an absolute determination on this point.

We now learn, however, that Richard has crossed the line into illegal sexual harassment, although he may have psychologically crossed the line much earlier. This difference between the legal and psychological "speed limit" confuses employers, who must decide how to effectively reduce the quid pro quo threat so that it will not become a major liability to the company. On which standard should the company set guidelines, the legal or the psychological measure? Very different prescriptions to employees on how to behave would follow accordingly.

Looking more closely at what the Supreme Court means in its definition of "conditioning employment to sexual favors," we see a curious thing. The conditioning of sexual favors can be paired to either the *granting* of employment benefits or the *denial* of current or future employment benefits. Was this only an attempt on the part of the Justices to make sure they included all the "weapons" a harasser has in his or her arsenal of supervisory power, or is there more reason to specify both potential forms of conditioning?

The inclusion of both forms is revealing of the psychological dynamics of quid pro quo sexual harassment. There is no hard and fast rule on how a supervisor harasser engages the target, but experience teaches us that most harassment couples follow a rather predictable course of action. It falls into two phases.

The *engagement phase* comes first. It can be described in terms of the activities the harassment couple agree to share, as expressed in the harassment contract. The *disengagement phase* begins when one member of the couple wants to break free. It can be described in terms of typical interactions that are common to the "divorcing" harassment couple.

Using this two-phase model, we can reorganize our perceptions of Richard and Crystal in the previous chapters. Their legal quid pro quo problem can be described in terms of our psychological model, and we can be clearer on what happened to them and why.

In the engagement phase, the supervisor attempts to seduce the partner with enticements of positive reward. Seduction begins with a "honeymoon period," when the supervisor is on his or her "best behavior." The goal during the first phase of engagement is to negotiate the harassment contract. Because both parties enter the contract "willingly" (if not always "knowingly"), it is quite unlikely that the term harassment will come into play just yet—*psychologically*. However, the *legal* prerequisites of quid pro quo are already present.

In Richard's case, his initial approach to Crystal is intended to be inviting and warm. He has high hopes for their shared future. Like many harassers in the honeymoon period of engagement, Richard is entirely unaware of the hostility that lies beneath his gestures of "kindness" to Crystal. Instead he sees himself as her "benefactor" in the corporation.

Crystal, like many harassment partners in the engagement phase, is confused by the mixed messages she receives from Richard. On the one hand, as noted earlier, she appreciates the "special" position she enjoys as one of his "favorites." The sexual favors that are demanded of her by Mr. Whatman are rather small, and the potential rewards are quite large. Although she apparently submits to Richard's requests in the beginning, Crystal, like many harassment partners, is uneasy entering a contract in which she accepts rewards that are not fully earned.

The quid pro quo contract between the harassment couple is sealed in the period of engagement. Whether the couple is securely or ambivalently attached, the contract is usually based on perceived positive rewards for both parties. The first legal assertion of quid pro quo sexual harassment is that it involves the demanding of sexual favors in exchange for favorable work conditions. This acknowledges the essence of what psychologically transpires in the period of engagement.

Incidentally, in another scenario, *Crystal* might have seduced *Richard* into the contract, rather than the other way around. If the subordinate proposes the contract to the supervisor and offers favors in exchange for special treatment, the supervisor might still be held liable if the subordinate has a change of heart.

Once successfully engaged, however, the harassment couple is set on a collision course. Regardless of whether sexual advances are welcome, the partner who submits communicates agreement with the contract to the supervisor. Therefore, as we have seen with Richard and Crystal, the terms and conditions of the harassment contract are likely to unfold freely.

Tension mounts. The less able the harassment partner is to assert herself or himself, the greater the resentment grows. The partner eventually starts to pull back, and the supervisor pushes forward to regain what is slipping away, until the point where the "traffic is more than the highway can bear." Usually, the partner ends the "honeymoon period" by trying to renege on the harassment contract.

The period of disengagement then begins. The terms and conditions of the work relationship shift dramatically for the harassment couple as the contract is altered.

Once spurned, the supervisor's concealed hostility surfaces. The easiest way for this individual to "punish" the harassment partner for the loss of attention is to fall back on the terms of the contract that have been violated. When Crystal withdraws her "favors," Richard withdraws his "rewards." Quid pro quo swings both ways.

So does the law; hence the need for the *second* half of the definition of quid pro quo sexual harassment: Rejection of advances is conditioned to *loss* of *tangible* benefits or denial of *future* opportunities.

The subordinate, previously a harassment partner, is now officially a "harassment victim." The supervisor, previously the holder of privilege in the harassment contract, is now officially a "sexual harasser." This labeling is from a *legal* perspective.

From a *psychological* perspective, however, nothing substantively has changed. An ongoing relationship has simply unfolded to its next developmental stage.

In the phase of disengagement, much as in divorce, the harasser is no longer "friendly" to the partner. Instead, he or she feels angry and betrayed. Richard has been empowered by Crystal's past acquiescence to his requests and is by now quite distorted in his notion of what he can "get away with." His greater authority in his work *role* only heightens his sense of entitlement over his harassment partner in their work *relationship*.

Crystal's wresting of control of the harassment contract away from her supervisor is a blow to Richard. She changes forever their interaction. Trust is broken. This is why Crystal comes to believe that she has "passed the point of no return" with Richard.

The law and psychology run on parallel tracks in defining the terms of exchange in quid pro quo sexual harassment in accordance with a shift from "honeymoon" to "divorce" of the harassment couple. Let us summarize those parallel tracks.

The Engagement Phase

🌿 Psychologically, the engagement phase, when the harassment couple forms, is a period of seduction. The harassment contract is drawn, and, during the honeymoon of early engagement, both parties see it as offering mutual reward.

🌿 Legally, quid pro quo sexual harassment is found if an employee demonstrates that sexual favors are exchanged for favorable employment conditions.

The Disengagement Phase

🌿 Psychologically, the disengagement phase, a period of renunciation of the harassment union, occurs when one of the parties reneges on the harassment contract. The harassment couple disengages, but not without anger and an increase in aggressive or retaliatory acts.

🌿 Legally, quid pro quo sexual harassment is found if an employee demonstrates that denial of current or future employment opportunities is conditioned to the refusal of sexual favors.

The Problems

1. When laid out in this form, it is easy to see why, most often, quid pro quo sexual harassment is not detected until the second phase of its occurrence, when one of the parties wants out and the other reacts defensively and punitively.

2. In the engagement phase, the behaviors that are *legally* sexual harassment may not be perceived that way

psychologically. Accordingly, to the harassment couple, the relationship does not become sexual harassment until somewhere in its mid-life, when the same behaviors that were accepted in the beginning are now illegal at the behest of only one of the parties.

3. This is inevitably a potentially litigious situation.

You may now be asking, "So what?" What Richard does to Crystal is unequivocally wrong, and the law *should* protect Crystal. That is reasonable in theory, but if this harassment couple's *legal* sexual harassment problem is only a fraction of their *psychological* problem, will punishing Richard help either one of them?

Let us review the facts of the case once more. In the engagement phase, Crystal's weak signals to Richard give him a green light to proceed in his negotiations of the contract. For a period of time, he is happily in the driver's seat. Riding high, he wants *more*. In contrast, Crystal feels increasing conflict at "giving in" and wants *less*.

Because of this pulling in opposite directions, the contract eventually rips apart and Crystal backs away. Her change of mind signals that disengagement is beginning. This hurts Richard and escalates rather than defuses his aggression.

Burdened by guilt and by the realization that Richard does not accept her breaking of the contract, Crystal gives up on correcting her situation. Her work performance suffers. Her feeling that there is "nothing left to save" may be more accurate about her self-worth than about her relationship with Richard, though it is doubtful she perceives it that way. Instead, she fights back against Richard's now discriminatory acts on behalf of her employment conditions, but this does nothing to restore her dignity or self-respect.

Crystal's anger is now displaced from her personal feelings about Richard's mistreatment of her to his manipulation of her concrete, tangible employment conditions. Crystal is in checkmate, but not at Richard's hand alone. She is a victim twice over: first, at her own hand, for giving up on herself in failing to resolve her psychological problem with this boss; and second, at the hand of her harassing supervisor, who also punishes her for their mutual troubles by unlawfully manipulating her tangible employment benefits. Crystal has nowhere to move psychologically.

A red light signaling danger should be switched on in the employer's mind at about this point in the story.

Crystal can move against this boss procedurally, if not personally. Her options are: bring a complaint forward to Human Resources, quit, or perhaps file a lawsuit against Richard and the corporation. These may remedy the harassment *symptom*, but they will not help Crystal recover from the harassment *problem*. The legal remedy does not satisfy the psychological need.

With the entirety of Crystal's feelings displaced into the arena of the manipulation of concrete employment conditions, would you want to be seated opposite Crystal on the defense bench in a court of law?

Let's look at Richard's side. Unknowingly, Crystal again underestimates her impact on Richard in delivering her despairing protest against his "punishing" performance appraisal. She tips the balance of power away from him when she confronts him, and she jolts Richard into the shocking realization that he has left himself vulnerable to her. More than hurt, Richard is now worried. He retaliates to rid himself of the threat of Crystal and becomes a full-fledged harasser who will do anything he feels is necessary to protect himself.

If nothing changes, Richard's options are equally grim. He can fire Crystal or railroad her into quitting through poor performance evaluations and undeserved criticism. But this would leave him *more* vulnerable to her retaliation. He will have then dealt her an economic blow in addition to possible psychological injury. She can contest his actions, and this could escalate into litigation. Richard too has placed himself in checkmate.

When seen in this light, Richard is also a victim. *Yes*, he has culpability in the harassment. *Yes*, he has supervisory authority over Crystal and he has abused it. But is he responsible for all that has transpired in the Crystal matter? In Richard's view, Crystal is not innocent of all complicity in this affair.

You may have already begun to realize that this case of sexual harassment is more than only a legal problem. At this late stage, there is little that we can recommend, for Richard or Crystal, that would stop the downward spiral of aggression and counteraggression that characterizes their quid pro quo sexual harassment relationship, especially if our attention is riveted solely on their overt acts. Thus far, the first line of defense—for these two employees—has failed to prevent the sexual harassment.

Call in the second line of defense: the corporation's anti-harassment policy and complaint procedure. If the individuals cannot stop the harassment, the problem is kicked up to the corporation to provide a remedy.

It is our wager, however, that the corporation too will fail.

This is a typical case where intervention to "stop Richard" will have only short-term effectiveness, if any at all, in correcting the problem. Human Resources may scare Richard into stopping his punishing acts toward Crystal, but this will do nothing to help the corporation's harassment problem.

On the contrary, punishment of Richard will not only *not* correct the problem at its roots, it may actually make things worse for the corporation in the long run. Richard will gain little from punishment alone, because he does not yet understand what he has done wrong.

Worse still, punishment, in Richard's current defensive state of mind, will add to his feeling of persecution and heighten his aggression. If put in emotional "lock down," he will have to hold in all of his frustration, confusion, and distress. The shame and anger left in the wake of the Crystal matter—the very emotions that made him a high risk for becoming a sexual harasser in the first place—will be stockpiled for later discharge. It may or may not take the form of sexual harassment, but this is not the last we will see of Richard's self-defeating behavior.

Relatedly, there is no guarantee that Crystal will accept or benefit from intervention by Human Resources at this point in time. She too is extremely conflicted about the harassment events and is confused by her mixed emotions and perceptions. She wants Richard's approval, is angry with him, and blames herself—all at once. Many victims, like Crystal, do not want help from Human Resources even when it is available to them. They may prefer to step outside the corporation to continue the fight against their harassers, rather than seek a remedy within the corporation to make amends.

You may wonder: What need is satisfied by keeping the war going? As psychologists, we suspect that, underneath the confusion, Crystal is deeply disappointed in Richard. But she does not know that, and that is a danger. If the second line of defense, the corporation, fails to stop the harassment, the case may be "kicked up" to the third line of defense. A court case looks very appealing to this victim.

This is a typical quid pro quo scenario. It is very serious not so much because of the severity of the harassment *acts*, but because of the enmeshed dynamics of the *actors*, who are unable to free themselves of the psychological conflicts that are played out through the arena of the sexual harassment *symptoms*.

THE PRESCRIPTION

If Crystal cannot bring the harassment to the attention of a friend, colleague, or other agent of the corporation, nothing can be done by her employer to help her. Were she to go to an attorney, she might have a chance of successful litigation, but the amount of punitive damage to the corporation would be militated against whether it had a policy and complaint procedure in place that Crystal *unreasonably* failed to use. Nevertheless, liability for Richard's sexual harassment is "absolute," and the corporation is responsible for his acts as a supervisor toward a subordinate.

What a dilemma for everyone involved! The law is unequivocal in its remedy for the sexual harassment *symptom* (Richard's final act of retaliation against Crystal), but it leaves untouched the deeper harassment *problem*. The corporation's only available remedy—stopping Richard by punishment—may suppress Richard's sexual harassment *acts* but is a stopgap solution at best.

Legal and procedural remedies take the corporation so far, but they cannot get to the roots of sexual harassment. The law targets only the *harasser* as the problem, for the obvious reason that his or her misconduct, unlike that of the victim, carries economic disadvantage. Richard can hurt Crystal professionally and economically in a way that Crystal cannot hurt Richard. The inequity that the law seeks to correct is *economic*, not emotional.

The law was never intended to adjudicate the *psychological* inequities of sexual harassment. Richard and Crystal are equal contributors to their psychological problem. Were they to exhibit the same behaviors toward one another outside the corporation, they would be held equally liable for the outcome of their relationship. Each plays a hand in the joint interaction, and each must therefore be a part of its remedy. When they come to work, however, the rules shift.

We are now one step closer to solution. The law can correct for the power disparity between supervisor and subordinate—often male and female, respectively—that gives advantage to the supervisor. It is left to the corporation, however, to realize its responsibility to go the rest of the distance to prevent sexual harassment.

To whom in the corporation does this responsibility fall, and relatedly, what exactly does *prevention* require?

Human Resources (HR) is the usual entity that shoulders these responsibilities. However, most organizations limit HR's function to the *legal* aspects of sexual harassment, such as receiving employee complaints, conducting investigations, and following up on sanctions that are applied against harassers. The HR unit is also responsible for training employees in using the company's antiharassment policy.

These functions are important but they deal only with the harassment *symptom,* and they are not adequate to address prevention. However, borrowing from the principles of psychology on preventing sexual harassment, HR can do a great deal more.

Much psychological research has been done on aggression. We can learn some important lessons from HR professionals who are confronted with solving the interpersonal and psychodynamic problems of sexual harassment in the workplace. These lessons may be organized around efforts to help the harassment couple and efforts to help the rest of the organization.

Regarding remedies for the harassment couple, research teaches us that when human beings are in a state of heightened emotional arousal, the nature and direction of their actions will be strongly influenced by their *perception* of the cause of their aroused state. The key concept is *perception* of the cause and not perhaps the cause itself.

Accordingly, in cases of the heightened emotional state associated with sexual harassment, the most immediate target of *perception* is the opposite half of the harassment couple. Each party is defensively blaming the other at the time a complaint is heard.

It is very important for HR counselors to spend time with each member of the harassment couple so that he or she can step back and allow the heightened arousal state to subside.

Only then can the employee be open to gaining deeper insight into the harassment dynamics and learning what happened from a perspective other than his or her own disappointment, anger, and hurt. This permits both parties to take responsibility for their part in the problem.

Human Resources needs to be available over a period of time, to give the employees repeated opportunities to talk about the harassment experience.

Too often, however, HR professionals are torn between the many demands to emotionally support the accused *and* the accuser in the harassment aftermath, *and* fulfill the executive function of objectively recording the complaint and conducting the investigation. Wearing two hats, as "judge" and "counselor," is extremely difficult. Because they are trained for the former more than the latter role, HR professionals may define their purpose too narrowly. They may see themselves as nonjudgmental data collectors on the harassment complaint or *symptom*; meanwhile, they are ignoring the *problem*.

We strongly advocate that HR professionals do *both*. Treating the psychological aftershocks of the sexual harassment and its investigation is at least as important to prevention as is handling the immediate formal complaint. If given no outlet for the heightened emotions associated with sexual harassment, the perception of both members of the harassment couple easily becomes fixated on anger toward the opposite party. Loosening negative emotions from their hardened perceptual target may be much more difficult later on, and the likelihood of litigation or other untoward consequences may be heightened.

To remedy the psychological harassment problem and aid in prevention, HR can take a second important step: education and training of the whole organization. Again, research on the impact of the social group on forming norms that prohibit aggression is most instructive on why this step is so important. It has been repeatedly shown that immoral and aggressive behavior can be stopped when members in a group confront each other about instances of misbehavior. When those who are troubled by aggressive acts remain silent, shared norms prohibiting the behavior do not emerge.

Accordingly, when group training in sexual harassment prevention focuses on psychological dimensions, it is most critical to the forming of a cultural consensus, within the corporation, that prohibits and later inhibits sexual harassment behavior. It is really quite simple: The organizational culture is the most powerful deterrent available to the corporation to ultimately prevent sexual harassment, but it is probably the *least* utilized tool.

Why?

We have been riveted on the *symptoms* of sexual harassment and on seeking *legal* and *procedural* remedies—the second and third lines of defense. We have diminished the importance of the first line of defense.

CHAPTER SEVEN

Don't Ask, Don't Tell
Won't Work

*Disengagement of the harassment couple officially begins
when one partner breaks free and brings the sexual harassment
to the attention of others in the corporation. The importance of
coworker empathy as the bridge that links psychology and the
law in the harassment aftermath is introduced. Empathy is the
core process that enables people to support one another in recovering from sexual harassment.*

After receiving an unfavorable performance review from Mr. Whatman, Crystal is more convinced than ever that there is nothing she can do to rescue her job. All that remains is saving herself. Until now, she has confided the sexual harassment to no one in the company. She is at her breaking point and cannot contain her emotions any longer. Crystal calls Jimmy, a trusted office friend with whom she can share her secret. She beseeches Jimmy to meet her for lunch. She needs to talk privately about the sexual harassment.

In the harassment aftermath, the corporation assigns various responsibilities to employees at different levels of supervisory authority. As we saw with Crystal and Liz, the procedural guideline that clarifies Jimmy's response, as a coworker, to Crystal's disclosure differs from the psychological experience. He struggles to balance the demands to be responsible to the corporation, sensitive to his troubled colleague, and true to himself.

THE SCENE

Crystal's shoulders were hunched over as she walked back to her office. The performance appraisal delivered to her by Mr. Whatman was still red-hot in her hand. She slumped into her desk chair and stared into space, trying to organize her thoughts. She wasn't entirely shocked by what had transpired, but she had sincerely hoped that it would happen differently and she would not have to face this moment of decision.

As Crystal reflected on her annual review, her anger became fury. "Mr. Whatman put his foot in it this time." She stood up and started to pace, talking aloud to herself, indifferent to anyone who might take notice. "Up until now, he has been nasty, *yes*; obnoxious, *yes*; critical of me at every opportunity, *yes*."

She did not know whether she was madder at Richard because he tampered with her promotion or because she was frustrated by her helplessness to get even with him. He had attacked her on an issue that she could not easily argue—her declining work performance. She could go up against him point by point, but to what good? Even if she was right on some of the issues, he was technically right on the others.

Crystal knew she was out on a limb. Mr. Whatman had pushed her there. She had to do something, but she did not know what that something was. She had to *think*. If she was going to fight back, she had to find out how to argue against an unfair performance review. She did not sign the document, so there was still time to write a rebuttal indicating her disagreement.

If she didn't do at least that much, what would Mr. Whatman do to her next? Her signature of agreement to the review would open the door for him to steamroller her again, whenever he felt like it. He could prevent her from being given a raise or a promotion—ever! How could she defend herself?

Crystal sat down at her desk and turned to her computer, intending to craft a defense to the objectionable review. Moments passed, but her fingers stayed inert on the keyboard. Her fury went up a notch at her inability to draft the document.

How dare Mr. Whatman put her in this position! This was all because of *his* misbehavior. It was entirely his fault.

Still, Crystal's fingers were motionless on the keyboard.

Crystal was too agitated to sit still in this state of writer's block. "Forget the rebuttal." She again started to pace. *Think.* Another alternative came to mind. Maybe she *should* go and talk to that counselor in Human Resources, and tell her what Mr. Whatman was up to. Crystal had never done anything like that before, and she didn't want to seem to be a "cry baby."

"Forget that, too!" she muttered aloud. Crystal knew why Mr. Whatman was punishing her. It was about nothing other than her refusing him his little "favors." But would HR believe her? No one had seen anything that had happened between them, or if someone did, he or she hadn't shared it with Crystal.

"Too risky." Going to HR was out of the question. "They'd believe *him.*"

Defeated, Crystal slumped back down in her desk chair. She thought about quitting altogether. Why stay and fight a losing battle? Crystal was in a bind and knew it. She needed a job, and quitting could indirectly compromise her future employment. She could not be sure Mr. Whatman would give her a good recommendation. In fact, she highly doubted it. He needed to have a "hook" to justify his misconduct, and her work had admittedly deteriorated. He would never own up to his part in why she had messed up those few times.

Crystal's head was spinning. She could not sort all this out by herself. There were too many unknowns. Crystal needed a friend. Almost without thinking, she picked up the telephone.

She knew whom to call; she had actually been considering this call for a while. She collected herself and took a deep breath as she dialed.

Jimmy worked in Information Technology (IT). Data entry and troubleshooting systems were his specialties. He had known Crystal since her first day on the job. American had employed him for one year before she came on board. Taking an instant liking to Crystal, Jimmy had appointed himself her guardian and mentor. He would show Crystal the ropes. Raised in a neighborhood adjacent to hers, Jimmy knew how tough it could be to get used to these "corporate types," who were very different from the people he and Crystal had known growing up.

Some days, Jimmy secretly admired Crystal. She had many qualities that he felt he lacked. Crystal had direction and a lot of drive. With that amount of ambition, he was sure that she would succeed at whatever she made up her mind to do. Jimmy was less sure of what he wanted, though he had a distinct talent for computers. He saw himself as only "marking time" in the corporation until he could decide on his ultimate direction in life. Jimmy was well paid by American for the work he did, and that compensated for the boredom and absence of challenge he felt. So long as Jimmy produced, no one much bothered with him.

On other days, Jimmy did not envy Crystal a bit. From his point of view, she was stuck in that "pressure cooker" of Whatman's sales and marketing operation. When he heard Crystal's voice on the phone, Jimmy thought it was just another one of those times when Whatman was on her case. She had been complaining of late that he was in her face more than usual and was "sharing" his troubles with anyone who couldn't get away from him quickly enough.

Typical Whatman! Typical Crystal! Jimmy shrugged. "This is why I have no prospects for success in the corporate world!" But Jimmy didn't care. He knew he was not made of the right stuff to put up with what Crystal took from Whatman, even if it meant he would never get ahead. Some things in life were just not worth the price you had to pay for them.

"Jimmy, can you meet me for lunch? There's something I have to tell you. I can't keep it to myself anymore." Crystal held her breath, waiting for Jimmy's response.

Jimmy knew Crystal pretty well. He could tell when she was really upset about something and when she was griping like everyone does now and then. This sounded like it could be serious. "What's wrong, Crystal?"

"You've got to promise me that you won't tell. I mean it, Jimmy. Not anyone." Crystal was surprised to hear apprehension creep back in her voice. She thought she had it under wraps.

Jimmy thought, "This *is* serious." Crystal was not herself. He wanted to calm her down. "OK, OK, Crystal, I promise. I won't tell."

This was going to be tougher than she thought. Crystal's stomach was in a knot. Telling Jimmy about Mr. Whatman meant taking a risk. She trusted Jimmy as much as she did anyone in the company, but once she turned the corner, there would be no going back. What if Jimmy slipped up and word got back to her boss?

"No, *really*, Jimmy. *No one*. You swear?" Crystal wanted reassurance.

"I swear. I don't work in your department, Crystal, so don't worry. I have no one *to* tell. What's this about?"

Jimmy did not know Mr. Whatman and did not have direct access to any of the people in Crystal's office. She had no excuse *not* to tell Jimmy. Crystal reminded herself that keeping the harassment secret did not help her with Mr. Whatman. That's what had gotten her into this mess.

"I'll tell you later. There are things going on." Crystal whispered into the phone. She would tell Jimmy the details over lunch, when they could talk in private. The office was not the place to share her tale of woe.

Despite her intention to exercise restraint on the telephone, Crystal could not contain herself. She blurted out, "I should've known it from the first day I started working here! What was *wrong* with me?" Crystal chided herself for her lack of self-control.

Jimmy did not understand what Crystal was referring to, though he clearly sensed that something was *terribly* odd about this conversation. Crystal was not one to hint around things, and she did not have a suspicious nature. Jimmy was puzzled and decided he had better have a talk with his protégé.

"You are full of mystery, Crystal. Let's go to lunch, *today*."

Crystal sighed with relief. The hardest part was behind her. She had taken the first step in letting Jimmy know that she had a problem.

"Great. I knew I could count on you. Jimmy, just remember—*you can't tell*. I don't want to lose my job. You know my situation."

Once again, Jimmy did not know what Crystal meant about his knowing her situation or about losing her job. Crystal lose her job? That made no sense at all to Jimmy. He could believe it of almost anyone else, but not Crystal.

"Yeah, Crystal. I know your situation, but obviously not *all* of it. I promise, I won't tell. What are friends for?"

Jimmy needed to find out what was wrong with Crystal.

Crystal finally stepped off the train.

THE DIAGNOSIS

Crystal is about to tell Jimmy about Mr. Whatman's sexual harassment of her. Jimmy doesn't know anything about it, and a beleaguered Crystal is ready to explode. It is not uncommon for events around sexual harassment to unfold in this way. The disengagement phase is the most usual time for harassment to be exposed. One of the parties has become distraught and is unwilling to go on with the status quo.

Disengagement is also a critical time for the corporation. The organization is most at risk *after* sexual harassment is disclosed. As people learn what has been going on, the company must begin the recovery process and mop up the mess left in the harassment aftermath. The eye of the storm shifts from the harassment couple to coworkers in the organization, who are now openly confronted with the harassment problem and must come to grips with the feelings and issues it raises.

Crystal takes the first step in initiating the recovery process. She breaks open the "family secret" of Mr. Whatman's harassment to a trusted and heretofore unsuspecting coworker. As you will see, the reactions of coworkers — including colleagues,

HR counselors, managers, and executive officers—to the harassment couple will be critical in determining whether the corporation will heal.

We can imagine Jimmy's dilemma. Crystal tells him about Mr. Whatman and the events that have transpired between them. She asks him to maintain her secret. Jimmy reacts with anger toward Mr. Whatman. He cares for Crystal and, as in the past, assumes a role as Crystal's protector. He also feels responsible for other unnamed parties in the corporation whom Mr. Whatman could be harassing.

If this scenario is accurate, then Jimmy will not like the bind he finds himself in. He may want to help Crystal by encouraging her to file a complaint against Richard. He may reason that this is the best course of action for everyone. Crystal, however, may refuse to act against her harassing boss. Is Jimmy bound by his employer to betray the privacy of his friendship to Crystal and report what he learns?

This is a typical entry point of coworkers into the harassment drama. When they first learn of its occurrence, they must make a decision about what to do. It is therefore a good place to begin to explore coworker dynamics in relation to sexual harassment.

If Jimmy is like most coworkers, his first step would probably be to consult the corporation's antiharassment policy. Jimmy would learn that managers *must* report known sexual harassment, but all other employees are *encouraged* to report it. Jimmy is not Crystal's manager, nor is he a supervisor in the corporation. Therefore, although the corporation would *encourage* him to report what he knows, it is not required of him.

Were Jimmy a manager, the situation would be different. Not only does federal law *demand* that supervisory employees report all known sexual harassment, but it also states that the manager need not have direct authority over either of the partners in the harassment couple. In some states, managers are personally liable if they do not report sexual harassment. This means that if it can be shown that a supervisor knows about but does not act to stop sexual harassment, the successful litigant can hold the supervisor personally liable in civil court.

The obligations set forth by the corporation for coworkers and managers to report sexual harassment are clear. But do they help Jimmy to solve his problem?

Only partly. Jimmy is not required to report. Crystal is afraid to go to Human Resources on her own. And the Crystal we have seen is quite unlikely to ask Jimmy's help to take formal action. Unfortunately, most of the harassment partners we have known are much like Crystal, and they commonly quit their jobs rather than report their harassers. They often have confidants in the organization, but, like Jimmy, the confidants are asked to keep the secret.

We do not yet know how Jimmy will respond to Crystal's confidence. Reporting known sexual harassment is not an absolute obligation of nonsupervisory employees, though it may feel like a moral obligation. Again, as we have seen earlier, the legal and psychological parameters drift apart, and employees are left on their own in making decisions about "moving targets."

To get a glimpse of how people actually solve the "Jimmy Dilemma," we asked a sample of employees: "What would you do if you were Jimmy at this point in the sexual harassment drama?" About half our sample answered that, if they were Jimmy, they would report the situation (before or after trying to convince Crystal to do so). The other half answered that they would not report. In the absence of a formal "rule," fully *half* of our respondents were not persuaded to act on clear-cut, supervisor harassment directed against a greatly liked colleague.

How do we explain this finding? It is hard to estimate underreporting statistically (we can't measure an event that didn't occur), but we do know that coworkers generally are unlikely to report sexual harassment.

Common sense dictates that the reporting ratio should be the other way around. Looking just at the numbers, there are inevitably many more coworkers who eventually know of sexual harassment problems than there are victims. Furthermore, because coworkers are not directly involved, particularly in supervisor sexual harassment, they should logically be the *first* to come forward and report. In cases of coworker harassment, others around the harassment couple should be able to form a protective circle because the impact is diffused and the victims often many. By definition, the creation of a hostile environment extends *beyond* the victim to the broader workplace. Accordingly, it is doubtful that coworkers are unaware of the hostility generated by a sexual harasser in their very midst.

Again, we are struck by the fact that coworkers are least likely to report sexual harassment of any subtype. Are they silent because of fear? Lack of loyalty to the company? Indifference to the suffering of others? Low morality? Why don't more people like Jimmy actively engage in a recovery process? More importantly, how can we help to make the focus in the workplace genuinely supportive and respectful?

From the Jimmy Dilemma, we conclude that we cannot attribute underreporting to an absence of rules. We saw earlier that a sexual harassment policy *alone* is not enough to make the victim feel sufficiently protected to report. Other supports are often needed. Could it be that coworkers, like victims, are afraid to speak out?

The reasons for Crystal's silence are complicated, as we have seen. Looking just on the surface, however, fear of retaliation by Mr. Whatman initially holds her back from telling Jimmy about the harassment. Fear of not being believed by Human Resources holds her back from filing a complaint. Fear of betraying Crystal holds Jimmy back from taking action against the harassment by reporting it to HR. Everyone appears to be afraid of *something*.

What triggers this chain of inaction?

We know from psychology that antagonizing an aggressor provokes aggression and therefore increases the vulnerability of the victim. We have already seen how this works between Richard and his victims—Crystal and Liz—when they confront him about his hostile behavior. Turning our attention now to coworkers, they too are instinctively reluctant to wave a red flag in front of the bull. The organization responds to this instinctive fear *rationally* by including in the complaint procedure a strong clause that prohibits retaliation against any employee who reports sexual harassment.

The corporation's procedural protections are unambiguous. Were Jimmy to read the company policy further, he would learn that it names the party responsible for receiving sexual harassment complaints, and it outlines the steps that will subsequently be undertaken. Human Resources makes a written record of all allegations and conducts an investigation for each one. The harassment parties named, and the witnesses, are questioned. Confidentiality is ensured to the greatest extent possible, and information is shared only on a "need to know" basis. And, most importantly, *retaliation against any person for reporting sexual harassment is strictly prohibited* and is punishable up to and including termination from employment.

These strong procedural safeguards are intended to assuage coworker fear. However, in actual practice, the law and psychology drift apart once more. The company policy says to the coworker, "You are protected." But, the coworker does not feel protected. With all parties knowing the right thing to do, trust breaks down and employees are disabled.

We begin to suspect that coworkers' reactions to sexual harassment are as complex psychologically as the reactions of the harassment couple, though they are far less well studied. Let's look at the factors that determine how coworkers form judgments about sexual harassment and how these factors affect their compliance to rules and procedures.

THE PRESCRIPTION

The organization promises protection from overt retaliation by angry harassers to coworkers who report sexual harassment, but coworkers are still reluctant to come forward, as seen in the underreporting problem. Based on what we know of the psychology of victims, we propose that coworker reactions may fit the same model. Their reluctance is also based on fear of retaliation if they support the victim. Reprisal of an angry harasser is often subtle and beyond the reach of Human Resources, especially if he or she is a powerful force in the company. The coworker who sticks his or her neck out on behalf of the harassment victim fears becoming the *next* victim.

If this is so, what is the psychological force that propels some coworkers—about half of our group—to support a victim in spite of this fear, but compels others to turn away?

Coworker reactions to sexual harassment are rooted in the psychological function of *empathy*—we began to explore the importance of empathy in relation to the harassment couple. Now its importance in predicting coworker responses to sexual harassment is explored.

Empathy is a special mode of perception that allows us to know another person "from within." Unlike intellectual knowing, empathy enables us to emotionally know others. It relies on our capacity to create an inner image of another person onto which we then project our own emotions. Through mutual interaction, emotions and observations are shared. A bond forms between ourself and another, and it enables us to feel close to that person.

Empathy is the main cognitive instrument for human communication and mutual understanding. It is formed of three psychological components that work together: (1) sensitivity, (2) perception, and (3) projection.

Sensitivity is commonly called "intuition." It is an innate capacity we are born with that enables us to sense the intentions and motives of others. It is purely emotional and does not rely on intellectual knowledge of a person. Lower animals even have a degree of sensitivity—as when a favored pet "knows" when its master needs comfort and sits by his or her feet in a gesture of support.

Perception is what we commonly call "insight." This second step in the empathy process occurs when information that is gained through sensitivity is combined with cognitive understanding. Through perception, we form an image of the other person "from within," and we can understand the motivations and intentions that define his or her inner self.

Empathy requires one last step. The products of intuition and insight must be connected to us emotionally if the experience of another person is to have meaning. Through a psychological process called *projection*, we put our own self into the inner image of the other person—an image we have created by combining our sensitivity and perception. We attribute emotional life to other persons by understanding them through the filter of our own feelings, not just our intellect.

When these three processes are integrated, we are able to empathize or "know" the experience of another while keeping our own identity and feelings separate. Without empathy, we cannot experience human closeness. Though it is constitutionally determined at birth, empathy is modified over the course of development. It begins in the relationship between infant and caregiver, and it grows through interactions with others later in the life span. Because it is a developmental process, it can be learned and changed by life experiences.

Understanding empathy is critical in preventing sexual harassment. It is the best available human protection against aggression. Under normal conditions, it is *impossible* to be empathically bonded to someone and aggress against him or her at the same time. Failure of empathy explains psychologically what occurs in the workplace when employees cannot bond together and use the resources that are made available to them by the corporation to protect themselves and one another against the aggression of a particular member of the group—in this case, the sexual harasser.

Our work on the perception of sexual harassment has shed light on how coworkers' capacities to empathize affect judgments about workplace behavior. When we asked, "Have you sometimes felt like [videotapes of assertive and nonassertive harassment victims]?" we consistently found that observers described themselves as feeling more like the harassment victims whom they saw as "stronger."

In short, when employees cannot identify with a victim, they cannot empathize.

Few people would want to put themselves in Crystal's shoes and identify with her experiences. This may seem irrational. It is hard to imagine a human being who has not felt as intimidated or helpless as Crystal when faced with aggression like Richard's. Crystal exhibits one of many common reactions to supervisor harassment. But just as common is denial of ever having felt that way! Helplessness, especially if extreme, is a feeling most of us like to *distance* ourselves from.

The particular ways in which people distance themselves from disturbing identifications with harassment victims (or harassers, for that matter) vary, but they are all instances of a derailment of empathy. And, as we have seen, a nonempathic coworker is unlikely to be of much help to the harassment couple or to the organization to which the couple belongs.

The failure of empathy can take a number of surface forms of expression, based on which of the three component processes—sensitivity, perception, or projection—is at the root of the problem.

If empathy failure stems from the sensitivity component, despite accurate intellectual understanding of the harassment situation, the person lacks the equivalent capacity to "read emotion" accurately. Though able to identify with the harassment couple, he or she makes wrong assumptions about their emotional context.

    ✺ This coworker may be seen as "trying to help," but because logic is filtered through a faulty emotional "screen," he or she will come to the wrong conclusion.

If empathy failure stems from the perception component, good intuition does not integrate with rational and critical reasoning. Judgments about the harassment couple are made, but the interpretation remains self-centered and the emotional boundary between coworker and harassment couple is lost in the identification process.

    ✺ This coworker fails to keep an appropriate distance between personal feelings and those attributed to the harassment couple.

If empathy failure stems from the projection component, sensitivity to the emotions of the harassment couple is present, as is accuracy in reasoning about their context, but understanding is limited to the intellectual level.

    ✺ This coworker sees the harassment couple "from within" and constructs the couple's context accurately, but stands apart emotionally and is therefore of only limited help.

These reactions of failed empathy are at the core of the psychological explanation of why coworkers often resist getting involved in a helpful way in the sexual harassment drama, despite a corporate policy that advises them on their role expectancies and protects them against retaliation in fulfilling these obligations. Addressing these roadblocks is central to enhancing the efficacy of coworkers as prevention agents in sexual harassment, particularly the hostile environment type. Coworkers have a critical task: to protect one another and create a safe environment in which to confront often painful recovery challenges.

Crystal has laid open the "family secret" of her relationship to Mr. Whatman. Liz has already taken Cathy into her confidence about Richard. The net is closing around our harasser as more people in the corporation learn of these events. As the story unfolds, you'll see the important role of empathy in predicting the reactions of coworkers toward victim and harasser. The coworkers make various attempts to mop up the mess and restore balance to the weakened corporation in the harassment aftermath.

The American Corporation is on the "critical list." Its chances for a full recovery lie not only with Human Resources and executive management, but also with the coworkers who are on the first line of defense in repairing the breach of trust that the sexual harassment and its aftermath have wrought.

CHAPTER EIGHT

Reasonable Person or Unreasonable Act?

You will explore the next condition of hostile environment sexual harassment, that harassing conduct is considered so by the reasonable person. This is the standard adopted for making judgments about workplace hostility. But it is a moving target, and it can be difficult for harassed employees to hit it with confidence. The whistleblower is therefore vulnerable to guilt and self-doubt, and coworker empathy is especially important during this phase of recovery.

*P*rior to now, the noose had been only loosely tossed around Richard's neck. He had not yet been apprised by anyone of the danger that could arise from his harassment. Liz takes another step to shake up the organization, and Richard receives his first rude awakening.

When last seen, Liz was unable to reframe her harassment problem with Richard in terms of their more pervasive work problem. Steeped in denial, Richard likewise could not move beyond the hostility stalemate. The situation had nowhere to go and could only get worse. Liz finally decides to file a complaint against Richard with Human Resources. An investigation is conducted, and Richard is asked by the corporation to relocate his office away from Liz.

With the harassment now out in the open, coworker reactions deepen in importance. The legal and psychological underpinnings of coworker empathy are explored further as Liz and Cathy attempt to support each other in their interpretation of what is reasonable. Liz discovers that agreement about Richard's harassment behavior is not enough to relieve her of the guilt she feels from having participated in the formal proceedings she initiated against him.

THE SCENE

Things can turn on a dime. Liz had been riding high for a while on the rewards garnered from her victory on the Redman account. She was "the one to watch" in the sales and marketing department. She had to admit, it felt really good.

Liz had developed a new confidence. She hoped she would not lose it as time went on.

Liz didn't kid herself, however. She never forgot that when the Redman secession was finalized, she could find herself back on the street. She had no guarantee of continued support with the incoming executive management. She eventually informed Mr. Griggs of her concerns so that her bases would be covered in the event that the new CEO at Redman chose not to renew the short-term contract with American. All she could do was wait and hold the reins steady until the critical period had passed.

Richard was not proud of his own thoughts, but he secretly hoped that Liz's coup with Redman would backfire. He knew this was not the *right* way to think, but he did not care. Liz had not exactly done anything wrong to beat Richard out of the account, but he could not shake the feeling that she had in some way tricked him. Her plan had been a whopping success in gaining Griggs's attention. Richard noticed that Griggs was more solicitous of Liz than he had been before. She had certainly won an advantage over Richard on this account.

All good things must pass. A few months after the executive takeover, Liz learned some unexpected and quite unsettling news. Redman announced that it would not renew the American deal but would reopen the bidding at the close of the current contract year. American was invited to resubmit. It was not the total disaster she feared, but it left her back at the starting line, forced to renegotiate what had been a stressful ordeal. Nor would she be through with Richard as soon as she had hoped.

Richard was jubilant at the news. He was not out of the game yet. His excitement was momentarily tempered by an awareness that he would again have to collaborate with Liz, and he remembered what trouble that had been. Nevertheless, he dashed off to find her the moment he read the Redman e-mail. He could hardly wait to see the look on her face when she learned that her "private deal" with Redman would be overturned and the race was on again, with the new CEO as the prize.

Richard found Liz sitting by herself in the lounge. A cup of cold coffee was untouched on the table before her. He sidled into the seat next to her, and she recoiled to gain some distance from him.

"Oh well, Liz, it looks like we're gonna be partners again," he said sarcastically.

"Isn't it just like Richard to be unable to contain himself when his good news is my bad news," Liz observed silently.

But she also noted that Richard sounded about as unenthusiastic at being her partner as she was at being his. This confirmed for her that the announcement to reopen bidding translated to a repeat performance of the competition, subterfuge, and hostility she and Richard had volleyed back and forth in the past.

Liz suddenly felt very tired, and Richard seemed lost in his own world. In a rare moment of honesty, Liz and Richard accidentally caught themselves staring deeply into each other's face, as if searching hopelessly for an answer to their mutual deadlock. Though unhappy with the stalemate, they did not know what else to do, and neither was willing to give in.

Over the next weeks, Richard and Liz met to plan strategy. Each would have protested that they were "trying our best" to get along with one another, but the old hostilities resurfaced. Before long, Richard resumed his obnoxious and offensive remarks. After a particularly tense week, at Cathy's urging, Liz went to Human Resources to file a complaint against Richard for hostile environment sexual harassment.

Human Resources conducted an investigation of Liz's complaint against Richard. She had been honest and told them everything, from the problems at the holiday party to Richard's many comments and snipes in the privacy of their shared office. Cathy had been named a witness, as were a few other women who had been at the holiday dinner dance. Based on the findings, HR issued a warning to Richard, and Liz was relieved of any responsibility that required working with him. Richard was taken off the Redman account because, until that time, Liz's signature was on the existing contract. Richard's offices were moved away from Liz.

Liz no longer had the "Richard Problem" on the coveted Redman account, but she lost the feeling of triumph she had enjoyed before accusing Richard of sexual harassment. She won the deal and she won the harassment case, but she felt as though she had somehow lost the war.

Liz poured herself into her work, hoping that if she kept busy, the time in the office would pass quickly. She felt sore from the ordeal of the investigation and was trying to recuperate. A knock on the door interrupted her intense concentration.

"Who *is* it?" Liz asked cautiously.

"It's *me*—Cathy. Let me in!"

Liz stood up slowly, opened the door a crack and peered through, to be certain it was Cathy. She was afraid of seeing . . . Who? She didn't know, when pushed to think about it. She was just extremely uncomfortable. How did her coworkers feel toward her in regard to the action she had taken against Richard? By now, she was sure everyone in the office knew about the investigation. Richard moved out overnight; by morning, he was gone. Too many people were now involved for Liz to believe for a moment that her complaint could be kept quiet.

"I'm glad it's just you." Liz motioned Cathy to come in.

Cathy entered and glanced around the room, taking it all in. Her eyes met Liz's. Her friend looked worried and distracted, and Cathy wanted to comfort her.

"Liz, you look beat. What's wrong? You've been holed up in here all day."

Liz was surprised that Cathy had to ask. It was hard for her to imagine that she, of all people, did not perceive the reason at once. But Liz needed to talk, so she decided to give Cathy a chance.

"Sit down." Liz motioned to Cathy, who accepted her invitation. "The investigation has been rough on *me*, too. Richard isn't the *only* one who has suffered. HR moved him out of the office last night. See?" Liz indicated the empty desk that was once Richard's. "He's gone!"

Cathy looked at the empty desk and felt a pang of guilt for the first time. She hadn't actually considered what would happen to Richard, or the effect on Liz, when she encouraged her friend to file the complaint with HR. Cathy had tried for so long to get Liz to make a move, and had been so disgusted with Richard, that she hadn't thought much about the aftermath. Now it was time to make it up to Liz.

"Relax, Liz, *I* think you did the right thing."

Cathy reached over and patted Liz. As she continued, she picked up her tempo in an effort to lighten the somber mood in the room.

"Anyway, according to the gossip mill, most folks are on *your* side."

"Yeah, I suppose *some* are," Liz replied half-heartedly.

Cathy's cheering words did not comfort Liz. Instead, they stirred up her worries once more. What repercussions would reporting the sexual harassment have on her reputation? She wasn't sure she wanted to know the secrets of the "gossip mill" just yet.

Liz puzzled Cathy. She never seemed to guess this friend correctly. If she were in Liz's place, she would be dying to know the office scuttlebutt on Richard. Not so, for Liz. Cathy waited for her friend to speak.

Liz took a risk and asked Cathy the question that was on her mind all day.

"Tell me, Cathy, how come *I* feel guilty for reporting *Richard* for sexual harassment? Almost like *I'm* the one who did wrong by telling on *him*. How did the tables get turned?"

"So *that* is what is bothering Liz," thought Cathy. She knew the answer to this riddle with no effort at all.

"It's to be expected, Lizzie. It isn't easy to be a whistle-blower."

Liz felt a hollowness in her stomach. She had not thought of herself in that light. Whistleblowers are people who take a courageous stand against injustice! Not wimps like her, who let people like Richard walk all over them first. She didn't know how to respond to Cathy's declaration.

"A whistleblower. . . . " Liz repeated Cathy's term in a whisper of disbelief.

Cathy couldn't understand why her second attempt to cheer Liz had no more success than the first. What did Liz *want* to hear?

Liz needed Cathy to understand her, though she hardly understood herself. Whatever Cathy was saying, in her effort to help, didn't feel right. Liz felt unsure of her own footing and preferred not to hear what her coworkers might think of her. She was surely no champion of women's rights!

"You know, Cathy, Joe is avoiding me, too. He used to stop by after lunch to talk, and now *he's* disappeared. I feel like I've become the office pariah!"

"*Why* do you care, Liz? For*get* it. *You* know that you are right!"

Cathy sighed in utter frustration. She was not succeeding at comforting Liz. Her friend *didn't want* the reassurance that her coworkers were on her side. She *didn't want* Cathy's sympathy. Cathy did not know what else to say.

Sensing Cathy's frustration, Liz grew defensive. She usually stopped talking when she felt misunderstood, but this time she was desperate. She didn't want Cathy to leave her office angry with her. Liz couldn't stand having one more person disappointed in her. She was already too disappointed with herself.

Liz pleaded one last time with Cathy to understand her situation.

"It's not that simple. I don't *dislike* Richard. I *do* believe he behaved abominably, but that doesn't mean I wanted to *destroy* him. Did I overreact?"

"I don't understand why you are feeling so guilty, Liz. You did *nothing* wrong."

THE DIAGNOSIS

Disengagement raises issues between coworkers whose resolve is critical to the recovery of the organization in the sexual harassment aftermath. Liz has taken another step in correcting the sexual harassment problem: She has filed a formal complaint against Richard. She acted in harmony with the corporation's antiharassment policy and Human Resources properly fulfilled its obligations. Only named witnesses were interviewed, in an attempt to protect the privacy of the harassment couple to the greatest extent possible. By removing Richard from their shared office suite, an appropriate step was taken to protect Liz from any discomfort or direct retaliation.

After all of this, Liz is still upset. She asks Cathy, did she overreact to Richard? Her concern is what others in the workplace will think of her. She reflects on her own uncertainty about the boundaries of perception and on whether she can expect agreement from others on her judgment of Richard.

The law on hostile environment sexual harassment advises us on Liz's concern. The criterion for judging the hostility of an act is whether a *reasonable person* would find it so. Judgments of severity and pervasiveness of harassment are considered from the perspective of the typical employee. Some states have modified this standard to *a reasonable person of the same gender as the accuser.* This modification refines the *reasonable person standard* to include finer distinctions that men and women have when they are deciding what constitutes sex-based offensive conduct.

The law therefore assumes that employees share a common normative value system that guides judgments pertaining to sexual harassment, and that even if we can't define all instances of it, we "know it when we see it." Further, it allows that although persons who report sexual harassment may feel a measure of "survivor's guilt," it is not based on differences in *perception.* As Cathy tells Liz, it is a "normal" reaction to "blowing the whistle." The guilt should pass if nothing further happens. If this is so, validation of Liz's experience by coworkers should be enough to assist her recovery.

We set out to determine whether these assumptions are true. First, and most important, is there a "reasonable person" standard that informs us on what most people will identify as constituting sexual harassment, and if so, on what is it based?

We asked observers to rate the level of hostility shown by the same harasser when paired with two different victims. The quid pro quo victim received verbal propositions, physical touch, and a poor performance review as retaliation for refusal of sexual favors. The hostile environment victim received only two verbally inappropriate remarks—far less severe treatment objectively than the harassment acts committed against the first victim. The two victims differed, however, in their reaction to the harasser. The quid pro quo victim was less assertive than the coworker victim, though, interestingly, neither was successful in stopping the harasser.

Did the observers rate the harasser as more hostile in relation to the quid pro quo victim or the coworker victim? Can you guess? Logic tells us that he was *in fact* more aggressive in relation to the quid pro quo victim. Would not a *reasonable person* concur that a supervisor's unwelcome physical acts, refusal of employment opportunities, and frank propositioning for sexual favors from a subordinate constitute *sexual harassment?* And, moreover, that this is more overt and blatantly *hostile* than clumsy and inappropriate remarks to a fellow manager such as, "Is it that time of the month?" Is there any doubt, objectively, which is worse?

Answer: The observers rated the harasser as more *hostile* in relation to the coworker victim!

What is going on? The law and psychology again drift apart. The law tells us that the reasonable person standard is sufficient to guide us in making judgments about sexual harassment. And that, in coworker harassment in particular, perceived hostility is based on the severity and pervasiveness of the acts committed.

The observers tell us that judgments of hostility depend not only on the *objective* acts committed but also on how we *perceive* those acts. Finally, this perception of severity seems to have as much to do with the victim's response as with the harasser's behavior.

We begin to get a hint about why Liz is not helped by Cathy's well-intentioned efforts to make her feel better by assuring her that her perception of Richard as a harasser is shared. She has most certainly taken into account the law of the reasonable person, but she has not taken into account the laws of human behavior, which pull Liz in another direction.

Liz feels guilty. We need a tool to build a bridge that will correct the gap left between the legal and emotional parameters in making judgments about sexual harassment.

THE PRESCRIPTION

What have we learned about the perception of hostility? For the observers, judgments on the severity of the harassment shown them were based not only on the acts committed by the harasser but on the perceived vulnerability of the victim.

In Chapter 4, we spoke about *blaming the victim* in relation to our anger toward Crystal for her failure to end her harassment problem with Mr. Whatman. We will now look at blaming the victim from another perspective and see how it can inhibit coworker empathy for a harassment victim.

Blaming the victim occurs when we attribute the cause of an act of aggression to the recipient rather than the aggressor. The misapprehension behind it is that the victim "must have done something to deserve it."

The psychology behind it is quite different: Blaming the victim is a special case of the failure of empathy. We remember that the observers also reported liking the assertive victim more than the less assertive one, and feeling more like the assertive victim. Simply put, human beings do not typically place a positive value on "weak" people and do not usually want to be like them. When confronted with passive victims, we tend to blame them for their misfortunes, as a means of creating distance between them and us. We do not want to project ourselves into their helplessness or victimization.

This is Cathy's problem with Liz, though in a disguised form. Her failure of empathy is not a result of lack of sensitivity. She is extremely reactive to Liz's plight and has been tracking her friend's harassment events with keen interest from the beginning. Cathy intuits Liz's moods and uses her sensory impressions to gain insight. Cathy is able to successfully integrate impressions of Liz to formulate an intellectual understanding of her "from within."

Cathy falls short on the final step of empathy. She is unable to project herself into Liz's experience. In the beginning of the scene, Cathy is attuned to Liz's feelings, reaches out, and offers insight into her colleague's situation. But when she is asked by Liz to identify with her feelings about the events, Cathy's empathy breaks down. She intellectually understands why Liz is upset, but she cannot "get right" with Liz emotionally. The solutions offered to make her friend feel better do not hit their target, despite Cathy's sensitivity and insight.

Liz knows that her conflict goes beyond rational factors and that "knowing the right thing" and "feeling right about something" are not the same. Liz is aware that she, too, can't "get right" with her emotions about her situation.

What is it that Liz and Cathy can't "get right" with?

The observers' responses tell us more. Liz is not irrational, as Cathy suspects, to hold on to needless worry about what others in the office will think. Perhaps Liz knows intuitively the psychological need to distance ourselves emotionally from victims.

Whether or not coworkers overtly blame Liz, emotionally they will probably look for something "wrong" with her that justifies the harassment, or they will build other defenses that say, in one way or another, "What happened to *you* couldn't happen to *me* because I am not like you!"

Cathy's failed attempt to be empathic to Liz reinforces Liz's belief that others will also judge her negatively for not being able to take care of the harassment problem herself. Though trying to support her friend and coworker, Cathy does the reverse, but does not know why. Cathy is Liz's best friend. It is not a stretch for Liz to imagine that if she cannot gain Cathy's empathic understanding, what can she reasonably expect from other coworkers who are less motivated to help her recover?

We must be reminded that Liz has not been successful in handling her interpersonal problem with Richard outside the sexual harassment. Now that she has gotten back at him through Human Resources, however true her allegations of sexual harassment may be legally, she knows that *all* of her problem with Richard is not his harassing conduct. Some of it *is* her fault. The investigation gave her an unfair edge in her race against Richard. She won the battle for the Redman account but she lost the war. Integrity is surrendered when victory is achieved this way.

This scenario is quite common. Sexual harassment is always only a part of a complex workplace communication. Victims of coworker harassment therefore often feel some complicity in the negative relationship in which the sexual harassment is encased. This does not excuse the harasser in any way, but it renders the victim vulnerable for guilt and self-blame in the harassment aftermath.

As we outlined earlier, the management of Liz's problem is not the concern of coworkers, but of Human Resources and other appropriate officers or counselors in the organization. The coworkers' role is only to support Liz. This may look easy, but experience tells us otherwise.

We have seen over a decade's worth of volunteer Cathys, in sexual harassment training sessions, who have brought great determination and enthusiasm to role-playing an empathic response to a volunteer Liz. Rarely, however, do we find one who does not fall into one of the many traps of misdirected empathy, despite good intentions. This occurs because of both a *healthy* unwillingness to project into the victim role and an unawareness of the subtlety of the harassment couple's contract and its associated guilt in the disengagement stage.

Failed coworker empathy will take a few common forms among even the well intentioned. Cathy is the first prototype, and her reaction is most common in relation to the victims of sexual harassment. We call this representative of failed empathy the *Coach*. Like Cathy, this coworker tries in some fashion to cheer up the harassment partner during the disengagement stage of recovery.

Coaching can take a number of forms. Promises for a better future as a reward for great courage are common. "Things will get better!" "You did the right thing!" "We're all proud of you!" are typical statements of a cheerleading Coach.

Another form of coaching is to minimize the emotional effects of the harassment on the victim through a showing of excessive sympathy. "We all want to help you!" "You look terrible! Why don't you take a vacation?" are among the sympathies offered.

A Coach cannot break free of his or her own feelings about the harassment, whatever form of expression they may take. Each of the above statements reflects coworkers' need to create distance between the victim's experience of guilt or loss and themselves. Sensitivity and intellectual insight are present, but projection failure prevents this employee from talking to the "within self" of the whistleblower. The harder the Coach tries to encourage the person to feel better, paradoxically, the less understood the victim feels.

Cathy wants to comfort Liz. Liz wants to be comforted by Cathy. Neither succeeds. Cathy cannot put herself in Liz's shoes. Instead, she puts Liz in her shoes and misses the mark in empathy. And Liz cannot overcome her guilt long enough to share with Cathy what she is truly feeling guilty about. Empathy breaks down, and an opportunity for recovery through communication is lost.

CHAPTER NINE

The Morning After

You will explore what happens to the accused after an investigation of coworker harassment is complete and the corporation specifies steps for restitution. You will step into the shoes of the harasser and experience what it is like to abide by the procedural requirements demanded by an employer while trying to maintain personal dignity and self-respect. The reactions of coworkers can greatly help or hinder the outcome during this sensitive time.

*Liz hides in her office in the aftermath of the sexual harass-
ment investigation. She is afraid to face the judgment of others
in the corporation after "blowing the whistle" on a fellow manager. She does not doubt her own opinions of Richard, but she
regrets that she needed to go through a formal complaint process
and could not solve the problem on her own.*

*Richard is moving into his new office. Relocation away from
Liz was one of the sanctions applied by the corporation against
him at the conclusion of the coworker sexual harassment investigation. Further, he has been prohibited from sharing an office
with another female manager for a probation period of no less
than six months. The only other male manager in the marketing
division is Joe, who was recently promoted and very much in awe
of Richard.*

*How will coworkers react to the defeated Richard? Under re-
strictions imposed by Human Resources, he may not talk about
the sexual harassment case. He is out on a limb, trying to effect
his own recovery.*

THE SCENE

Joe arrived in his office early to make sure he got in before
Richard, who, he heard, was moving into his suite today. Joe
had moved into the office only five months earlier, when he
was promoted to a management-level position. Richard was a
legend, and his name preceded him within the corporation.
Although they were in the same marketing division, Joe and
Richard were layers apart in rank, and Richard's arrival was
"big news" for Joe.

Joe straightened up his room, making ready for the arrival of the marketing superstar. First impressions were important, and he was nervous. The great disparity between Richard and himself made Joe uncomfortable. It was unusual for the corporation to pair managers who were this different in rank, and Joe wondered what reasoning was behind the executive decision to move Richard in with him.

Joe was also uncomfortable because of the first and last brief one-on-one encounter he had had with Richard some five months ago. Just after he received his promotion, Richard had stepped into Joe's office to welcome him to his new position. Based on Richard's reputation, Joe imagined him a charismatic man who commanded respect—an authority by anyone's call. Instead, he had been surprised and confused by Richard's offhand and hostile remarks about the corporation.

Joe had worked indirectly with various members of Richard's team on two or three projects since that chance meeting. Though his contact with him was only from afar, Joe had not again found himself disappointed in Richard. He had indeed shown himself to be the business leader and innovator that Joe had imagined him to be. But he couldn't entirely shake the memory of the "Welcome aboard" speech, either.

Joe was puzzled. *Did* Richard have another side? Could that have gotten him into serious trouble of one kind or another? If so, did it cause him to suffer a fall from grace? In that case, the move to Joe's office would be a "punishment" for Richard and hardly a coup for Joe.

Joe doubted this line of reasoning. Richard would have had to have done something really serious to be cast from so lofty a perch. Joe had not heard of anything of the kind.

Joe considered another hypothesis to explain the move. Richard might have been asked by executive management to move for a reason connected with Joe. But this probability was still slimmer. Joe could not think of any *good* reason to pair Richard with him. Joe was doing well but was still getting his feet wet. He had not distinguished himself to the point of earning recognition as a candidate for grooming by a superstar.

And realistically, why would *Richard* move to *his* office and not the other way around? Any such explanation was a pleasant fantasy and nothing more.

Looking at his situation yet another way, Joe considered whether he had done anything to raise an eyebrow of suspicion that might warrant any special monitoring. Could that be why Richard was moved in by Maintenance in the middle of the night, when no one was around?

Joe did not know what to think. Human Resources had only advised him that Richard would be moving his office because of some "restructuring," and informed him of the date of relocation. Joe hoped that when Richard arrived he would find an answer to the puzzle.

As Richard pulled his car into the parking lot, he braced himself for the ordeal that lay ahead. He knew that once he got past the initial stares and whispers, it would get easier. He had deliberately given little thought to preparing speeches. No one was allowed to know about the sexual harassment allegations made by Liz, other than those who participated directly in the investigation. They included Cathy, two women from the administrative pool (who accused him of inappropriate behavior at the holiday party), and, of course, Liz herself.

Richard was not naïve, however. He figured that he would also have to reckon with a gossip factor. These women were all friends, and Richard believed that they had ganged up on him to help Liz out. They corroborated her story to Human Resources and added a few tidbits of their own. Richard could not accuse them of lying, exactly, but if his comments and gestures had been such a bother to them, why did they wait until Liz filed a complaint to suddenly come forward and plead their case?

Richard was certain that more people than just those directly involved in the investigation knew about the sexual harassment complaint against him. He could only imagine what Liz and the others were saying, and how people received their storytelling. Adding to his discomfort, he was not supposed to talk about the case to anyone in the company, or so Human Resources had strictly advised him.

This posed a special problem for Richard. He felt defenseless against unidentified rumors and possibly malicious gossip. Human Resources had tied his hands and, for the first time in a long while, Richard was helpless. He could not protect himself. It seemed quite unfair to him that he was prohibited from talking about the sexual harassment under threat of dismissal for retaliation. If Liz (or anyone else, for that matter) chose to break the confidentiality rule, however, and talk about *him*, no harm would come to them.

The complexities and inequities of this situation frustrated Richard. He understood that he was the identified culprit in this hostile environment accusation, and the corporation expected him to pay a price for the "harm" he had caused Liz. But he didn't agree. To Richard, it was just another ploy on

Liz's part to get at what he had. In another day and time, complaints such as these would be taken with the grain of salt they deserved. *So what* if she didn't like his sense of humor. What does that have to do with business?

Richard would use the gag order from Human Resources to protect himself from the embarrassment of public humiliation about this messy situation. He could hide behind the restrictive clause, too. If no one was supposed to know, so be it. "Mum" was the word. But he was still outraged that the gag order also left him vulnerable to covert malevolence from coworker gossip.

Richard decided that the best course of action was to proceed as if nothing had happened. He was relieved that most of his things had been moved by Maintenance the night before. He was ready for a fresh start. The next rite of passage was greeting Joe, his new roomie.

Richard was conscious of his gait as he strode into Joe's suite, carrying a last box that contained his personal effects. He held his head high and threw his shoulders back, greeting Joe without a moment's hesitation.

"H-e-y, Joe. Looks like you've got a new roommate."

"Welcome." Joe matched Richard's greeting and added nothing more.

Joe reached over to help Richard clear a space for his things, in a nonverbal show of welcome. Richard nodded, placed his box down, and unpacked his few belongings. Joe busied himself as Richard settled in, which did not take long.

An uncomfortable silence filled the room as each man apparently waited for the other to speak.

Joe broke down first. "I was pleased, but also surprised to find out you were moving in here."

Richard responded to Joe with a forced, terse smile. He felt dismay that his new roommate seemed to be taking a direct route. Not that Richard wouldn't be that way himself, if the circumstances were reversed. Joe was a manager and was naturally curious about the politics behind Richard's abrupt move.

Richard was beginning to feel trapped. He had warned Human Resources that it was ludicrous to think it sufficient to tell Joe his move was part of a "restructuring of the department." No manager would buy that lame excuse.

Richard was right. When Joe heard Richard's mumbled reiteration of "restructuring the department," he knew Richard was holding back. This intensified Joe's concern that something important might indeed be going down in the corporation, something he would want to know more about.

Joe pushed the envelope a little further. Not wanting to make it sound as though he was making any negative assumption about Richard, he phrased his next question carefully.

"How'd you fix the move?"

This was ridiculous! Richard could not keep up the lie and allow Joe to think that stepping down from his suite in executive row into *this* office was something Richard had "fixed!" Any fool would guess otherwise.

"Well, it wasn't entirely *my* choice." Richard folded his arms defiantly across his chest.

He hoped that Joe would back away, but this was not to be Richard's luck.

"No? Whose decision was it?" Joe's curiosity had peaked. What was the hidden agenda in placing Richard in *his* office? Maybe he *was* chosen by executive management for leadership development. That would be welcome news.

Richard had no idea what was going on in Joe's mind. It hadn't ever occurred to him that Joe might be thinking about himself. Richard's only thoughts were about what Joe might know about *him*.

With Joe rooting about for information, Richard worried that maybe he had fraternized with the gossips. Did Joe know about Liz's accusation of sexual harassment? If so, how could Richard sit back day after day not knowing what Joe had been told—or what lies Joe believed—about him?

This was not a tolerable situation for Richard. "You haven't heard?" he asked.

"Heard what?" answered Joe.

Richard thought for a moment, but only for a moment. He would begin slow, sharing only the bare bones of the matter, and wait to learn what Joe knew. Forget confidentiality!

"Liz filed a sexual harassment complaint against me, and the next thing I know, HR does this investigation and I am told I need to move out of my old office suite, away from Liz. I guess they took her side."

Joe fell into his chair. He was prepared for any one of a number of possible reasons for Richard's move, but this was not on the list. He was dumbfounded and speechless.

Richard could feel Joe's shock. He hadn't known anything about Liz's complaint after all. Richard relaxed, thinking to himself that maybe Joe could be won over and he would have an ally in these hard times. It was worth a shot.

To hell with the gag order! There was no way he could work in such close quarters and not say anything in his self-defense. It was unreasonable to expect it of him.

"It's just as well they moved me. There is no way we could work in the same suite now that she's 'ratted' on me!" Richard just *knew* that Joe would understand.

Unfortunately for Richard, Joe was not trying to understand Richard but was worried for himself. He wondered what the relocation meant in light of this new discovery about Richard. Why had management moved him *here?* Was there a message to be deciphered?

To Joe, this was beginning to look less like preferential treatment by executive management than its opposite. When did his office become the dumping ground for the corporation's waste?

"You had better mend your ways, ol' boy!" Joe's feigned boyish charm sounded watery thin, even to himself.

THE DIAGNOSIS

Richard has been treated in accordance with the corporation's antiharassment policy and its complaint procedure. Liz reported Richard for sexual harassment. Human Resources conducted an investigation. Reasonable effort was made to protect the privacy of Liz, the witnesses, and Richard himself. A positive finding of coworker sexual harassment was reached. Corrective action was taken; in this case, it included the separation of the accuser from the accused. Richard was issued a warning; if he sexually harasses again, he will be immediately dismissed. He was also warned against retaliation, intimidation, or reprisal involving any of the employees who reported him for sexual harassment or who participated in the investigation.

This is a common scenario in cases of relatively mild coworker sexual harassment, where no economic or significant psychological harm has been found on behalf of the complainants. The courts do not require immediate dismissal of employees like Richard, who have been accused of actions similar to those described by Liz.

Liz follows the rules. Human Resources acts properly. Richard accepts the terms and conditions of his reinstatement. But what a mess! Liz is hiding in her room, struggling to overcome her guilt. She fears being labeled "the office pariah" for blowing the whistle on a colleague of equal rank, whose actions she now believes she *should* have been able to handle herself. Joe is confused and upset when he learns the true reason for the arrival of his new, once-esteemed office-mate. And Richard feels trapped between his natural instincts to take care of himself and a corporate policy that prohibits him from doing so.

The disengagement period is now in full tilt. Neither the harassment couple nor the coworkers around them feel secure or protected, yet the corporation, in acting responsibly in this sexual harassment, has done *everything* "by the book."

In earlier chapters, we started to look at the reintegration issues confronting the harassment victims and their coworkers during the disengagement phase. We saw that more than policy and procedure are needed to effect an enduring recovery in the organization. We also showed why empathy is the bridge between the law and psychology, and is the central factor in the healing process.

We now turn our attention to the harasser. Richard has been yanked out from behind his screen of privacy. The harassment is now "above board" to selected individuals in the corporation. He, too, must face his coworkers and reintegrate into the organization in the aftermath of the investigation.

In this phase of recovery, the corporation must procedurally enforce its protection of Liz (against potential retaliation by Richard) for reporting sexual harassment. Among the protections offered, all parties in the investigation are placed under a gag order. They are not to discuss the harassment with others in the workplace. But only Richard is under threat of punishment if the gag order is violated in a way that can be construed by Liz as retaliatory. Thus, the strictest restraints to open communication are placed on Richard.

But Richard, perhaps more than anyone, has the greatest *psychological* need for constructive communication about the harassment in the reintegration period. Instead, we find him "walking on eggs," not sure who knows what about him in this very sensitive matter. In this scene, he must face Joe, not knowing what he will say. Until now, Joe has been a distant coworker who has had only the highest regard for Richard. This is an awful lot for Richard to cope with.

Joe is also in a quandary. How can he possibly be of any help in the recovery process when he is not even privy to the harassment? We call Joe and Richard a "double-blind" harasser–coworker pair. *Neither* member of the dyad knows what the other one knows—yet they must in some way come to terms with reintegration.

Joe has been "set up," in a way, by the corporate policy. The gag order does not protect him; it actually makes matters worse. He was unaware of the true circumstances of Richard's move. When he learns the truth, "Lucky me!" becomes more like "Why me?" and he loses heart.

Richard is walking into a psychological trap, and he knows it. You may argue that he deserves this punishment as the just result of his prior disregard of Liz. Too bad for Richard! It is his turn to suffer.

But Richard's suffering will do no good for Joe, Liz, or anyone else. The corporation's policy and procedure have been followed. They may serve the employer's goals of physically protecting Liz and shielding the corporation from liability against Richard's coworker harassment, but they do not serve those "in the trenches" who must somehow march forward in the harassment aftermath.

What would help Richard make the transition back to productive work relationships in this stage of disengagement?

Imagine that the scene between Richard and Joe happened exactly as described, but Richard was being reprimanded for something other than sexual harassment, something that was not unlawful. What are the psychological needs of a recovering employee who feels stripped of dignity or has "lost face" after personal flaws were uncovered?

Richard would be free to talk to Joe (and others) in accordance with his comfort level and the degree of trust developed over the course of their relationship. Joe could make a decision about Richard independent of any deeper implications for his career because of which side he is on in the sexual harassment war.

Unfortunately, none of this happens. Procedures that are intended to protect employers and employees may fix one part of the problem but create another. When Richard's bad behavior becomes unlawful behavior, a new set of demands is placed on all parties. A problem that starts in human interaction ends up in a court of law. The playing field is no longer even, and the team is disturbed from engaging in its usual maneuvers. It must negotiate new boundaries of interpersonal communication.

All of this hampers the healing process. Some of the things that Richard or Liz or Joe or Cathy might *like* to do or say are not permissible. Richard tries to "stick to the rules" and keep quiet about the sexual harassment complaint, but this is out of character for him, and, with a little provocation from Joe, he lets loose.

Does this surprise you? Richard is not one to sit back in any situation that challenges his authority or prestige. This is one of the characteristics that make him a successful businessman. Should Richard, or anyone else, endure the intrusion of a manager of lesser age and rank who thinks he "has something" on him?

Again, the law and psychology drift apart. Any hope of Richard's getting help from Joe during his recovery is lost, and Joe's empathy for Richard is derailed.

But the rift goes deeper. Not only do the laws designed to protect squelch a process that is necessary to the healing of all parties in a harassment drama, but the harasser must endure an added indemnity. Again, our work on the perception of sexual harassment is instructive.

We asked observers to rate our harasser as presented in this book in five successive videos that showed him in relation to two different victims and one coworker. In the beginning, although they immediately perceived the negative traits in the harasser, our subjects granted him the benefit of the doubt when they made judgments about his character. Once they realized, however, that he was most definitely a harasser, they developed a negative mindset about him. From that point forward, no matter what the harasser actually did, the observers were fixated on seeing the "bad" in him.

We tried to dissuade these observers from their negative mindset. We described a list of other qualities the harasser had, and the positive activities he engaged in: being generous to friends and colleagues; being a top earner in the company; mentoring colleagues who are in need of advice; and being a hail-fellow-well-met and the life of the party.

Would this information modify their opinion?

What do you guess? Once he was perceived as aggressive, the observers refused to change their impression of the harasser, or his character, in order to see "the good" in him. Nothing else he did was of any import nor could it undo their negative impressions.

This response sheds light on an important psychological principle. We perceive some behaviors as reflective of a person's inner *traits*. Impressions are formed about the person's character, which we then view as unchangeable. Once an aggressor, always an aggressor. Other behaviors, such as assertiveness, for example, we see as *states*. We accept that these behaviors can be learned, or may appear and disappear according to the situation we find ourselves in. They are not fundamental to character.

This distinction between traits and states has very serious implications in understanding why it is so difficult for an organization to effect a successful recovery after sexual harassment has occurred. It may also explain why sexual harassers are often seen as having only low, if any, prospects for rehabilitation. We simply do not see aggressiveness as a dimension of human character that can be easily changed.

Joe's reaction to Richard can also be better understood in this light. When Joe learns that Richard is a sexual harasser, he reorganizes his entire perception of Richard around this information in a way that cannot be easily modified by subsequent experience.

Joe has become like one of the observers. Nothing Richard says or does is evaluated in a neutral light, as it was before. Though troubled earlier by Richard's aggressive "Welcome aboard" speech, Joe was still able to give Richard the benefit of the doubt. Maybe it was just an off day, and not indicative of Richard's true character. Subsequent business dealings corroborated for Joe that he was correct to afford Richard high regard.

Enter sexual harassment allegations and everything changes for Joe. Unfortunately for Richard and Joe, unless something else happens at this point in time, we would predict that Joe would become fixated in his distrust of Richard. He and Richard may superficially patch things up, but they will not overcome the insult of this breach. Joe loses out on a potentially productive work relationship with a senior colleague. He also loses faith in the organization that he once hoped would advance his career. Proximity to Richard now associates

Joe with the sexual harassment, and he feels victimized by being singled out to house a persona non grata.

What is the prognosis for Richard's rehabilitation? If he is in the same kind of bind with other coworkers that he is with Joe, it is not a leap of faith to predict that he is not long for employment in this corporation, and that he will leave with no more insight or self-control than he had when he came. His disappointment may be expected to harden into anger.

In training sessions, at this point in the drama, we often ask employees how they rate Richard's rehabilitation potential. What do you think we usually hear?

If you respond that most employees give Richard a "thumbs down," you are correct.

Given this same information, how do psychologists rate Richard's chances of recovery from the "problem" that underlies his harassment behavior?

If you respond that most psychologists would say Richard might very well have a good prognosis for recovery, you are correct. Recovery depends on a few critical factors, but not all harassers are incurable.

Richard's *psychological* problem, however, in the case of sexual harassment, is also a *legal* problem. He is forbidden to use his natural emotional resources to engage coworkers in an effort to mend the breach of trust and the break in communication that has been wrought by the sexual harassment.

Further, Richard's aggressive behavior happens to fall into a category of human experience that *most* people find very difficult to "get beyond." We are afraid and unforgiving of perceived aggressiveness.

It begins to look as though multiple forces, *legal* and *psychological*, conspire against the recovery of the harasser in the postinvestigation phase.

THE PRESCRIPTION

Experience teaches us that one of the single most powerful predictors of Richard's success at reintegration in the corporation will be his coworkers' response to him. Richard's ability to gain the support of important colleagues and create an atmosphere in which recovery is possible will determine his prospects for continued success in his employment with this company, and perhaps his personal rehabilitation as well.

This brings us back to empathy. What lesson can be learned from the unfortunate, but typical, exchange we witnessed between Richard and Joe?

We described empathy as requiring three things: (1) sensitivity, (2) perception, and (3) projection. We saw how a failure of projection caused Cathy to push Liz away rather than engage her. Joe's derailment of empathy for Richard has a different root.

Let's briefly look at Joe before he learned the reason for Richard's move. He does not seem to be a notably sensitive guy from the start. He is focused, ambitious, and driven, and he analyzes his work relationships from a self-centered perspective. He is also honest and does not seek to deliberately hurt others or take what is not earned.

Joe is not by nature especially open. He does not "tune in" to the feelings of others, and he is generally insensitive to moods and subtleties. This serves him well in the corporation because he is able to avoid many of the daily irritations that distract some employees from reaching their goals. Joe does not come to work to make friends. He comes to work to make money.

Joe is perfectly expectable as a prototypical employee. Though naturally low on sensitivity, he is still capable of developing *some* empathy. What happens when he learns of Richard's sexual harassment?

Like the observers, Joe develops a mindset about Richard and goes "over the edge" in his attempt to distance himself from him. We call a person who has this type of empathy failure a *Saboteur*. Unable to intuit the feelings of Richard (or anybody else, for that matter) Joe is left only with self-concern as a guide for his behavior.

Joe does not see an immediate benefit to himself from Richard's relocation. He therefore does not view this circumstance positively. In his role as a Saboteur, Joe unwittingly undermines himself *and* Richard by his unwillingness to look at Richard "from within." Instead, he prematurely gives up on Richard and distrusts the corporation for its perceived "mistreatment" of him.

Were Joe less fixated on himself, he might realize that the corporation's choice of his office as Richard's new location has nothing to do with him at all. Joe is simply the *only* male manager who has room to house a disenfranchised Richard.

Joe's emotional abandonment of Richard is going to cost him dearly. If nothing changes to repair the breach of trust between these two men, Joe will miss out on a very special opportunity.

Richard is at a critical juncture. At this point in the drama, he is about as fragile and defeated as we have ever seen him. Joe fails to appreciate how badly Richard wants and needs his help. It is extremely difficult for employees like Richard to accept being in a "dependent" role in relation to anyone. But if you have read carefully, you recall that Richard admitted inwardly that he secretly hoped to build an alliance with Joe.

In all these pages, have you yet heard Richard so much as *hint* at wanting or needing help from anyone?

At this phase of the harassment recovery, there is often a "window of opportunity" for reaching even the most recalcitrant harassers. If the Saboteur were to consider Richard's worldview, he might find that he could make a trusted, lifelong friend within the corporation.

Instead, empathy fails and Joe deserts Richard. Sadly, Joe does not know that he is the ideal person to help Richard begin his climb out of the harassment snake pit. If Richard has the type of personality dynamics found in most harassers, getting professional help is still very threatening at this point in time. His wounds are fresh and he is too afraid.

Joe is just the right distance from Richard to be of help. He is not too close personally, and his lower rank might encourage Richard to venture out and test the water with him, in an effort to establish trust. Richard and Joe both lose out. Joe is unable to be empathic toward Richard, and Richard is too ashamed to advocate for himself in building their work relationship.

We need not spell out what this failure of empathy predicts for Richard's recovery or for the success of the corporation's effort to mop up the mess.

CHAPTER TEN

Recovery Starts
at the Top

*You will explore how the reactions of executive officers spear-
head the recovery process of the whole organization. Leadership
bears two roles in the treatment of sexual harassment. It
is both the supreme representative of the organization and also
an employee in the organization. In its struggle to balance liability issues against personal feelings, leadership articulates the
organizational response to sexual harassment. If it fails, the
breakdown in empathy hurts the whole corporation.*

$\mathcal{R}$ichard's reintegration into the corporation begins on moving day, when he relocates his office to Joe's suite, the only available management spot that does not require shared space with a woman employee. Richard and Joe have a tough time getting beyond the awkwardness of Day One, and neither is able to successfully ferry himself through the transition phase. They build a wall of defense against one another.

One last step is required of Richard by his employer. He must meet with his supervisor, Mr. Griggs, to review the outcome of the sexual harassment investigation. Griggs has been CEO of the company for over a decade and is now closer to the end than the beginning of his tenure. He is required to engage an employee problem he has not directly encountered before. He especially regrets that the particular employee accused happens to be Richard, a manager of considerable financial value to the company, and one for whom Griggs also has high personal regard.

THE SCENE

This was very trying, very trying indeed. Richard did not care to devote so much emotional energy to worry over the opinions of others. Joe proved himself to be quite a disappointment. He could have seen the good in sharing his office with Richard. Even though Richard hoped the move would only be temporary, Joe should have been more welcoming. Instead, he seemed decidedly uncomfortable around Richard, almost as though he did not want him there.

Richard was sensitive to this rejection. He quickly withdrew any promise of camaraderie with this junior manager. On Joe's first visible sign of discontent, Richard slammed the door shut on Joe permanently, putting an invisible but impenetrable barrier between them.

Joe accepted Richard's dismissal of him, almost with gratitude. Not knowing what to say about the sexual harassment, Joe did not see a way to proceed after learning the real reason behind Richard's move. He was hurt, angry, and distrustful about the decision. It did not occur to him that he was the *only* male manager with whom Richard could be paired. The corporation's choice of Joe had no personal meaning to be deciphered, though he did not know this. Poor Joe suffered in silence.

With the breach in trust not repaired, Richard and Joe were in no condition to begin a new work relationship. But Richard's ill fortune was not to end here. His alienation deepened. Richard was scheduled to meet with Mr. Griggs, his supervisor and the CEO of American. He believed that this was just a formality, a follow-up to reinforce the seriousness of the findings of the investigation. However, this was the first (and Richard hoped, the only) time that he and Griggs would go face-to-face on the harassment problem.

Richard was grumbling. First the "interrogation" by Human Resources. Then, having to apologize to Liz. Next, having to explain himself to Joe. And the final ignominy? Having to recite a litany of mea culpas to his boss. What would come next?

"Liz pulled a fast one with this sexual harassment thing," moaned Richard. There seemed to be no end to his public humiliation. Richard had tried unsuccessfully to imagine how the meeting would go with Griggs, but he had no template to begin to construct such a ridiculously uncomfortable event.

Mr. Griggs suddenly felt very old. He, too, dreaded this talk with Richard. As he steadied himself for the encounter, his thoughts drifted to the beginning of their work relationship. That went a long way back. Richard had distinguished himself in Griggs's eyes from the start. He was ambitious, willing to take risks, and not a complainer. Griggs liked that, and accepted in Richard the good with the bad.

The "bad" aspects of Richard led Griggs to privately categorize him as a "high-maintenance top performer" who, despite his personality quirks, made it to the A-list when it came to results. Griggs rationalized that all his peak performers over the years came with some baggage. Why not Richard, too? He was temperamental, headstrong, and a bad sport when made to play second string. Griggs had to admit he had been a bit like Richard himself in his younger days.

Griggs longed for the old times, when men like himself—the CEO, for goodness' sake—were not asked to muddy their hands in messes like this.

"You ask me *why* has there been so much turnover in my department? HR has sent up the *wrong* people. *That's* why!" Richard repeated Mr. Griggs's prior question.

He wondered, was this supposed to be a "Richard-bashing" session or a serious talk about Liz's sexual harassment complaint? Richard's temper was rising, but he knew better than to make a show of it to Mr. Griggs. He was in a vulnerable enough spot already and could ill afford to bring more negative press onto himself.

Yet Richard could not help but feel picked on by his boss, who chose *this* time to confront him on Crystal's quitting as his administrative assistant. It must be Gang Up Against Richard Day. First Joe, and now Griggs.

Richard hustled to answer the CEO's query about his rate of staff turnover. Griggs was not privy to what happened between Richard and Crystal, or how Richard felt about her abrupt and unexplained exit. Crystal was just another fair-weather friend who had no loyalty to Richard in the end.

And *this* is what Griggs wanted to talk about? Not Liz? So be it! On second thought, Richard would rather answer the allegation about staff turnover than talk about the accusations made by Liz.

"Look at the last two administrative assistants HR sent up! Neither one was right for the position. Was it any *wonder* they left?"

Mr. Griggs considered Richard's statement. He had not known either of the women well, and perhaps Richard was correct. Backing off, he replied to Richard, "You *may* have a point there."

Mr. Griggs paused. He couldn't avoid the topic of Liz any longer. But in that split second, Richard thought that he might escape the "sexual harassment talking-to" after all.

Seemingly without any warning, the CEO impulsively broke into a trot. "But what about the complaints about *sexual harassment*? Now *really*, Richard, these allegations reach all the way upto *me!*"

This was not what Griggs had meant to say.

Richard returned the volley to safe ground in making his reply to Griggs. He continued on about the turnover in his office staff.

"I can explain all this. About my staffing problems, I am doing the best I *can* with the material I have been *given*."

Griggs did not interrupt Richard to bring him back to the task at hand. He was secretly relieved Richard did not pick up on the harassment issue. The relief did not last long, however. But now it was Richard's turn to succumb to the impulse. He launched an unnecessary self-defense.

"And about those harassment complaints, sir, I believe I have been entirely *mis*understood. I am certain things will simmer down now that I have moved my office." Richard did not allow so much as an ounce of emotion to show.

Mr. Griggs did not know what else to say. He was stumped. Richard sounded confident, positively confident! He had not expected this.

Griggs was unsure. He could not predict what Richard would do in the future. He liked Richard. But he was angry with Richard. And he felt sorry for Richard. Yet he also felt betrayed by Richard. He didn't understand Richard. Nor did he know whether it was his place *to* understand this aspect of Richard.

Mr. Griggs was in a muddle.

"I give wide discretionary berth to my managers, Richard. You have the freedom to run with the ball, but when I hear repeatedly that you have been *dropping* it, there is little I can do to help you."

Richard knew dismissal when he heard it. And it seemed to him that, of late, he was hearing more than his share of it, from just about everyone he came into contact with. And now from Mr. Griggs, too. As apprehensive as he had been about a confrontation with his mentor, Richard realized he was actually a bit disappointed that Mr. Griggs did not want to talk to him more about his problem with Liz.

"Whatever is the source of your difficulties, Richard, attend to it!" Griggs gave his final word.

"Yes, sir," replied a dejected Richard, as he stood up to leave the room.

Griggs stared at Richard as he walked away. He had second thoughts and almost called him back. Then he thought better of it. Instead, the CEO picked up the intercom and buzzed his administrator.

"Mary, please get General Counsel on the line." Griggs guessed he had better look into the Richard matter a little further. Protecting the corporation *had* to be his first obligation, no matter what he felt personally for Richard.

THE DIAGNOSIS

The course of an organization's recovery in a harassment aftermath is set by its executive officers, who define the path that others will follow at all levels in the corporation. How does leadership fulfill this special function?

Leadership has two jobs to do in sexual harassment recovery, as compared to others in the organization who have only one. Leaders represent the *institution*. They are standard-bearers *first*, and people *second*. We are less concerned with the personality of our leaders than we are with the integrity with which they carry out their responsibilities. We entrust to them our safety and security, and therefore require them to be fair-minded and dependable, above all else. Liking a leader is less important than trusting a leader.

Leaders, however, are also *people*. They form a special class of coworker; they are a functional part of the workforce of the organization. They form relationships with others that are based on their personalities. In this aspect, they are no different from any other coworkers. They will have a host of emotional reactions to sexual harassment, depending on their personal history and their degree of direct involvement with the protagonists.

Leadership's response to sexual harassment will therefore depend on its capacity to perform in these jobs. As the standard-bearer of the organization, the leader adopts formal procedural guidelines to protect employees against sexual harassment. These are embodied in the corporation's antiharassment policy and rooted in federal and state laws. As an individual, the leader's personal reactions are bounded by his or her capacity to empathize with the harassment couple, just as we have seen with respect to any other type of employee.

The nature of the empathic reaction of the leader, however, contains one critical dimension not operant for any other employee group. This derives from the special authority leadership has in making procedural decisions. Leaders *enact*, while other employees only *react* to, antiharassment policy. Therefore, leaders' level of empathy defines the quality of the organizational response to sexual harassment.

How does this occur? How do the *personal* capacities of the leader translate into the *organizational* response to sexual harassment? You may disagree with this assertion altogether, arguing instead that the *law*, not the whim of the *leader*, binds the corporation's response.

Let us review the dynamics of Richard and Mr. Griggs as a case study on the way in which the *procedural* and *personal* aspects of leadership interact in predicting the *organizational* response to sexual harassment in the recovery stage.

In our drama, Mr. Griggs has two sets of responsibilities that run parallel to one another in handling the "Richard Problem." First, he must concern himself with the protection of the corporation against any potential liability to which Richard is exposing it. This is his *procedural* obligation. Second, because Richard is also his direct report, Griggs must contend with a *personal* relationship with Richard.

Looking first at the procedural side, what is the employer's liability for Richard's behavior? Were our drama to continue, General Counsel would advise Mr. Griggs on the corporation's risk. The law imposes strict liability on the employer for quid pro quo sexual harassment. It is responsible for the creation of work conditions and is therefore responsible for any changes that are delivered by quid pro quo harassers.

Employer liability in hostile environment sexual harassment is more difficult to determine. The general rule is that if the employer can show that (1) it exercised reasonable care to prevent sexual harassment through an effective policy and complaint procedure *and* (2) the harassed employee unreasonably failed to take advantage of corrective opportunities afforded, an affirmative defense is allowed.

Mr. Griggs is not yet fully aware of the extent of Richard's harassment problem. He knows only of Liz's coworker complaint. The corporation took prompt and effective action in relation to Liz's accusations. An investigation was conducted, and all parties involved were informed of its conclusions. Corrective measures, including separation of Richard from Liz, have been carried out. Richard has been issued a warning, and he has been urged to see the counselor from the Employee Assistance Program, as we learned at the beginning of the book.

The corporation has met more than minimal *procedural* obligations to remedy Liz's sexual harassment complaint. Griggs, as procedural leader and standard-bearer for the corporation, has done enough.

Do you think so?

We usually take a poll at this point in the drama, when we are conducting training sessions. We ask employees: "Do *you* think the corporation has done enough in its response to Richard's harassment of Liz?"

Most people respond with an emphatic "NO!" They are still angry with Richard, and they feel the employer should do *more*. Mr. Griggs should *dismiss* Richard, or *demote* him, or give him a *reduction in salary*.

They call for *more punishment*.

This is a curious finding. In point of fact, all we have seen Richard do in relation to Liz is make a few inappropriate remarks about "that time of the month" and the shampoo she is using. We have also heard reference to his being seductive when intoxicated at the holiday party. Does this seriously warrant *more* punishment?

You may argue that we are dissuaded from reason because we have acquired a mindset about Richard based on other information. We already know of his harassment of Crystal. We are therefore predisposed to make a harsher judgment on Liz's behalf.

We thought so, too, and tested this hypothesis out. We showed observers the harassment story in reverse order, with Liz first and Crystal second. Do you think the judgment of Richard in relation to Liz changed?

No! The verdict from the jury was the same: *More* punishment!

The law and psychology once again drift apart. As a "procedural leader," Griggs is A-OK. As a "people leader," his dissatisfied constituency still wants revenge!

If you were Mr. Griggs, how would you evaluate the correct treatment of the Richard Problem? The law leaves a gray zone that executive decision makers must negotiate in determining what to do with a harasser like Richard, who has been accused of relatively mild coworker hostility.

Some corporations boast a "zero tolerance" policy for any and all forms of known sexual harassment. Others call for "progressive discipline" of relatively minor offenders.

Imagine you are Richard's employer in the fictional American Corporation. How would you decide on the best course of action to take, knowing only what Mr. Griggs knows of Richard's sexual harassment of Liz?

You might argue that it is to the company's best advantage to rehabilitate Richard rather than punish him—for a few reasons. First, he has value to the company as a producer, and replacing him could bring great financial loss to the corporation.

Second, the standard of *zero tolerance*, while noble in concept, may be rather severe in actual practice. Do you really want to terminate *all* employees reported for coworker hostility? If you lead a large and diverse multinational corporation, demanding uncompromising adherence to *any* set of rigid behavioral rules may be virtually unenforceable. You may be inadvertently inviting even lower morale and accusations of "unfairness" when rules are not uniformly applied to all.

Third, you may wonder whether severe punishment serves anyone's best interest. Liz will have even more trouble overcoming her guilt for "ruining Richard's career," and a record of termination for sexual harassment will permanently scar Richard.

Fourth, from a legal perspective, Richard has rights and protections, too. The decision on which sanctions to apply against him in relation to Liz's accusations will also be affected by the terms of his employment and the boundaries set by legal precedent.

For all of these reasons, and perhaps some others too, you decide that rehabilitation of Richard is the best alternative to pursue.

On the other hand, what if this decision is wrong and Richard "acts up" again? Will this constitute a failure on your part to protect your employees from a known sexual harasser? Looking at potential risk another way, how many times have companies been sued by accused harassers who file countersuits against their employers for unfair treatment?

Case law advises on appropriate *procedural* responses to sexual harassment, but its interpretation in actual practice, especially in cases of hostile environment episodes, is often a gray zone. Richard's hostile acts against Liz can be redressed by the corporation in any one of a number of ways and still be within the boundaries set by law. How do you decide which way to go? Punish or rehabilitate?

Our drama is a good example of the very real dilemmas executives often face. Griggs has only a limited set of facts about the sexual harassment problem, as is often the case. You know more about Richard's actions than Griggs does. You know that Richard's harassment has gone beyond verbal hostility and seduction, while intoxicated, toward a few coworkers. And legal counsel advises that if Griggs were to learn of Crystal's experiences, absolute liability would be attached to the employer.

Logic and procedure have taken Mr. Griggs only part of the way in effective decision making. What other cues did he have that might have led him to a better understanding of the problem or could help him to protect other employees, and the corporation, from sexual harassment?

THE PRESCRIPTION

Based on our experience, the capacity of executive officers to effectively reduce the risk of sexual harassment rests not on the law and policy, but on the personal characteristics of leadership. This may seem a radical assertion, but we maintain that if the CEO is too angry, blocked, defended, or otherwise indisposed, empathy will be compromised. And this will affect the company in many important ways, including whether there is a work environment in which sexual harassment is not tolerated.

The model used earlier to explain empathy on a personal level can be extended to explain organizational behavior in response to sexual harassment. More importantly, we can establish a link between the empathic capacity of the leader, in particular, and the creation of the corporate culture. You can then appreciate, for example, how the empathy failure of Mr. Griggs led to ineffective decision making about Richard, and a lost opportunity to safeguard the corporation against further harassment problems.

From our consulting experience, we have found that there are two kinds of organizations—empathic and nonempathic—just as there are two kinds of people. Sensitivity, perception, and projection—the three processes that define empathy on an individual level—also describe what leaders create in the corporate culture.

In the empathic organization, leadership expresses *sensitivity* as awareness of employee needs and attunement to what workers require to function effectively within the structure. Leadership expresses the second level of empathy, *perception*, as the capacity to translate impressions of employee needs (gained though sensitivity) into policies and standards to guide workplace behavior. Leadership expresses the third level of empathy, *projection*, as a willingness to commit the organization's resources to maintaining an atmosphere that supports the goals and standards articulated through sensitivity and perception.

Applying this sequence to sexual harassment, an empathic leader is *sensitive* to employee needs, both concrete and interpersonal; *perceptive* about how to monitor and identify breaches in expected behavior; and willing to *project* resources in employee education, training, and staff development to prevent sexual harassment. When a leader has good empathic capacity, these functions are exercised regularly, and the result is reflected in the culture. The organization is safeguarded against abuse.

The nonempathic organization fails at any one or more of these three levels. An organization whose leadership lacks *sensitivity* will ignore employee needs. Workers in this company will feel unimportant and not "listened to." When empathy failure is on the level of *perception*, leadership may sense an employee need but fail to articulate the standards and practices that will satisfy it. When the failure is on the level of *projection*, leadership may accurately identify and articulate an employee need but refuse to allocate the necessary resources to meet it.

Applying this model, we may now revisit Mr. Griggs. The hypothesis put forth is that his *personal* failure in empathy is transferred to the *organization* because of his key status as a leader. His shortcomings are no greater than Joe's or Cathy's, but, because of his executive position, they cost the company a great deal more. Had Mr. Griggs been more empathically attuned to Richard, he might have heard the many cues that were given, and that would have taken the corporation in a different direction.

If Cathy is the Coach and Joe is the Saboteur, we would have to name Mr. Griggs the Ostrich. Cathy's empathy derailed at the level of projection; Joe's derailed at the level of sensitivity. Mr. Griggs would appear to suffer a failure at the level of perception. He is quite intuitive about Richard's emotions and has formed an impression of him "from within." He can project himself into this image of Richard's experiences. He can see the similarity between himself as a younger man and those aspects of Richard that he senses.

What prevents Mr. Griggs from transforming *intuition* of Richard into *insight* into Richard's motivations and intentions?

A failure of *perception*. Recall that coworker sexual harassment is usually judged not on the basis of the hostility of acts but on *perception* of the intentions that motivate acts. What a disadvantage Mr. Griggs bestowed on himself by blocking out insight into Richard's *intentions*.

Mr. Griggs is not all that unusual. Leaders are under more pressure today than ever before. Poorly performing CEOs are three times more likely to get fired than they were a generation ago. Institutional investors, who own more than half the equities in U.S. corporations, relentlessly demand results. Whatever CEOs used to hide behind has been blasted away. And we want Griggs to be empathic!

The greatest cause of failure of CEOs, however, is lack of success in placing the right people in the right jobs, and the related failure to fix "people problems" in time. Mismanagement of the human resources of corporations has led to more failures than any other single cause.

Griggs is unable to deal with Richard, whose poor supervisory performance can deeply harm the company. Griggs has some inner awareness of the problem because he refers to Richard's high rate of staff turnover and his difficult personality. But he refuses to acknowledge the *connection* between the two—driven by perception—which is the same *connection* that would cue him into Richard's potentially serious problem with sexual harassment.

Sadly enough, Griggs is talking indirectly to Richard about the underlying problem that has given rise to *both* his sexual harassment and his high rate of staff turnover. But Griggs doesn't allow himself to "know it," and therefore cannot harness the awareness, gained through intuition, to true insight into the Richard Problem. Insight is a necessary precursor to effective decision making. Griggs's lack of *perception* disables him as a leader.

What pulls this CEO away from using his sensitivity to build empathy for Richard?

Griggs does not want to *perceive* the implications of the Richard Problem because it challenges his leadership in a way that is threatening. He does not want to see that he is vulnerable to the performance problems of others, like Richard, over whom he feels he has little control. Griggs instead invests blind faith in selected employees. We saw this earlier, when he let Richard snow him on the Redman account.

Through a process of avoidance, the Ostrich has stuck his head in the sand and does not see how Richard's character flaws connect to the corporation's sexual harassment problem. Instead, Griggs has misplaced a great deal of faith in Richard. Having become a victim of intellectual seduction, he overcredits Richard's talents and persuades himself that failure is not an option.

Mr. Griggs sounds awfully much like Richard a few chapters ago, when he recited one and the same mantra about himself. Are these two men in collusion on a level beyond their immediate reach?

This Ostrich is not just any coworker, however; he's the CEO. His failure therefore will also impact on how the organization mobilizes its response to the sexual harassment. Unfortunately for the American Corporation, Griggs's failure to acknowledge the seriousness of the harassment problem will result in a nonempathic organization.

Imagine what each of the characters you have met would feel under the leadership of this Ostrich CEO. We will make a few predictions, based on companies we have worked with.

❧ **Richard:** He will be contrite for a while and keep a low profile. But he will stockpile resentment over the losses he sustained in stature and friendship because of the sexual harassment investigation. Eventually, he will leave the company. American will lose a top performer. Richard's sexual harassment problem may or may not follow him elsewhere.

❧ **Liz:** She will eventually come out of hiding but will feel it "wasn't worth it after all" to have endured the punishment of reporting sexual harassment. After feeling like the office pariah, she will slowly segregate herself with the colleagues who gave her support, and distance herself from others who did not. She will never again feel the trust she once had in her employer.

❧ **Crystal:** See you in court! After leaving the corporation, she may seek external counsel to evaluate her case for litigation. Win or lose, if she discloses the harassment in court, we need to modify Richard's predicted outcome. He'll probably be fired.

❧ **Joe:** He'll stick around for a while and if a better job offer presents itself, he'll leave the company. He feels disillusioned by his employer and is burned up over the way he was handled. Joe feels deeply disrespected.

❧ **Cathy:** She's the best off, so far. She will still believe that Liz did the right thing. Accustomed to battle to get what she wants, this is just "another day." Cathy is tough. She is a fighter. Sexual harassment is not reason enough to make her quit. She will become the historian of the corporation.

If Mr. Griggs were to correct his empathy problem and pull his head out of the sand, he could effect a much better outcome. By gaining true insight into the situation, he could formulate a plan to not only heal the breach in trust that the harassment has wrought but actually improve the conditions that led up to the harassment symptom in the first place. This type of thinking helps to prevent future problems, as well.

These are among the steps that the CEO should take:

1. Evaluate Richard more closely, to make a better determination about his sexual harassment problem. This is often done by external consultants, who are in a neutral position to interview *all* affected parties and assess the causes, not just the symptoms, of the harassment problem. Recommendations for changes are made to correct the root problem.

2. Provide a vehicle for employees to talk about their feelings. This can be with external or internal consultants, or Human Resources counselors. When sexual harassment occurs, there is a serious breach in trust—not just between the harassment couple, but with others who are aware of its occurrence and are indirectly affected by it.

3. Provide training to the whole organization. This should be done routinely, but especially if an incident is reported. Sexual harassment is a red-flag warning; something is amiss in a culture that allows abuse. Training sends an important message that executive management cares about the enforcement of anti-harassment policy and, when an employee's rights are

violated, the corporation will not sit back. This protective attitude filters down to coworkers and gives them permission to also form a protective circle when others are in need of help.

4. Initiate executive management's direct participation in the training and rehabilitation activities within the corporation. For maximum benefit, it is important that all workers believe that the corporation has *one* value system and a shared commitment to cultural change.

If these steps were followed by Mr. Griggs, how do you think the employees you have met thus far would fare in the fictional American Corporation?

EPILOGUE

The real sexual harasser on whom this story is based spoke these words two years after his colleague filed a coworker sexual harassment complaint against him:

> I am a sexual harasser. After all this time, those words still sound as though they belong to someone else. I do not see myself like one of *those people*. You can't imagine how humiliating it is to be publicly labeled. In my case, when in the office, I went along with the corrective actions demanded of me by my employer, but quite frankly, in my private thoughts, I didn't believe it for a minute.
>
> The most difficult part of recovery was admitting I had a problem. Even after I was reported for misconduct, I still denied that my behavior was abusive. You see, I was never really angry with the women I was accused of harassing! To abuse someone, shouldn't you at least be angry with her? I actually looked forward to letting off a little steam by joking

around with the women in the office. Or so my thinking went.

When I was accused of sexual harassment, I felt as though it was *I* who was being attacked. I naturally responded by defending myself. I'm not proud to be saying this, but it took the threat of losing everything of importance to me to open my eyes. I hope others aren't as hardheaded as I was.

Sexual harassment goes unchecked in many corporations until it is too late to stop what could have been a correctable problem. This is because the critical players who drive its outcome—the harasser, the harassed, and their colleagues—miss their moment and do not act in time.

In this book, we have tried to "slow the speedboat" by uncovering the antecedents to sexual harassment in the preceding interpersonal events. At each stage of the drama, we offered prescriptions for intervention to all parties involved. These prescriptions applied not only to those directly engaged in the harassment acts, but also to colleagues and executive officers who surrounded the harassment actors. We saw that these indirect players often held the greatest power to shape the harassment outcome.

Our case illustration also dramatized the escalation of a harassment problem in the aftermath of its identification and investigation. This is typically the most vulnerable time for the corporation: factions form, resentments build, disgruntled employees climb on the bandwagon of discontent, and other complainants step forward.

Taking into account the bigger picture, we now revisit the question: What exactly do we mean by *prevention* of sexual harassment? Do we mean preventing a problem between two employees from fulminating into bona fide sexual harassment? Do we mean preventing a harassment problem from escalating to litigation? Do we mean preventing a recurrence of a harassment problem? Or do we mean putting our time and money into developing employees who can protect themselves from harassment before it starts?

If only one thing is clear to you by now, it should be that sexual harassment is *always* a complex problem that entails interplay among the law, psychology, and corporate policy. The problem does not start with the harassment act. It begins with complex workplace exchanges that occur over a long period of time. Where we define its beginning will determine how we see its prevention.

We have argued that it is most beneficial to you and to your organization to look at sexual harassment as a human problem before viewing it as a legal problem. This allows us to think about prevention before harassment starts. Procedural guidelines are necessary to protect employees from unfair employment practices, but, alone, they are not enough to prevent workplace hostility. People do not change internally because of external constraints.

The good news is that no matter how thorny or difficult they seem, employee relations are never set in stone. There is always room for growth. Therefore, in the most profound and enduring sense, prevention rests in your hands. If you are open to learning, enhanced empathy is a powerful tool to strengthen your immune system against workplace aggression, in whatever form it takes, gender-based or otherwise.

Understanding how to intervene in suspect workplace interactions before they fulminate into frank hostility allows us to alter the course of events and to prevent sexual harassment in particular. Workers at all levels of employment have a hand to play.

The importance of coworkers in preventing sexual harassment is often overlooked. This may be because we have traditionally viewed sexual harassment as a problem that belongs *only* to the harasser and the harassed. Yet, when we broaden our view of sexual harassment to include all of its associated events, before and after its identification, a very different picture emerges.

Coworker response is perhaps most critical to the recovery of all involved. When coworkers can respond empathically to the harassment couple, it is possible to prevent the secondary damage to the workplace that results from distrust in management's handling of the problem, and split loyalties between the accuser and the accused.

Executive leadership, a special group of coworkers' participation, has also been seriously overlooked as a prevention agency. When leadership is empathic toward the harassment couple, it views the harassment act as a buoy that marks a deeper conflict beneath the surface of the organization. From our consulting experience, we have learned that when an organization elects to look at sexual harassment as a symptom and as the problem itself, growth and increased respect and productivity always result.

If executive leadership is not empathic to the harassment couple, it surrenders a major opportunity to help employees regain a sense of job security or feel protected. In the absence of this opportunity, they will scramble for shelter, lose faith in their employer, and maybe even leave. These hidden "costs" of sexual harassment may be great in the long run. And even if immediate action is taken on the sexual harassment complaint, it is likely that future problems—harassment and others—will plague the company.

Next, we come to the harassment couple. What can they do to protect themselves? By "slowing the speedboat," we were able to appreciate that much of what transpired interpersonally between Richard and his harassment partners, Liz and Crystal, was due to misunderstanding. These misinterpretations escalated in accordance with the expectations and prior experiences each player brought to the table.

We hope we have helped you to think about your own biases and blind spots so that you know a little more about what *you* bring to the table. This will help you to think differently about suspect or hostile workplace interactions and what you can do about correcting them.

You are the first line of defense against sexual harassment.

APPENDIX

Field Manual:
Identifying, Reporting,
and Monitoring
Sexual Harassment

This appendix puts the finishing touches on how to protect yourself from sexual harassment. We respond last to the request people always make first—*Just tell me what to do!* Drawing on prevailing wisdom in the field of sexual harassment training, we guide you on what to do if you believe you, or someone you know, is being sexually harassed in your workplace. This is when knowing the do's and don'ts is important.

Unlike the approach taken in this book to prevent sexual harassment before it formally crystallizes, traditional training follows a crisis intervention model. It comes into play *after* a problem has already developed. It includes the term *crisis* with good reason. If nothing else is apparent thus far from reading our dramatization of Richard, Crystal, and Liz, it is that their explicit "sexual harassment" problem began long before it surfaced in the corporation. By then it had reached crisis proportions.

This is unfortunately "business as usual." It is true of *all* of the cases of sexual harassment we have encountered in corporations. By the time Human Resource or other management professionals learn of it, the harassment has been in progress for quite some time.

In acknowledgment of the sorry fact that prevention is not always possible, it is important to know the do's and don'ts. First, call *all* workers to the table—supervisors, nonsupervisors, and executives—any of whom can become partners in a sexual harassment couple, and each of whom play a role in responding to the potential harassment of others.

The do's and don'ts are formally spelled out in your corporation's sexual harassment policy. Most employees we have questioned over years of training report to us that they do not know if their company has a policy, and if so, they do not recall reading it.

We encourage you to take the time to ask your employer for the policy guidelines that govern employee relations in your workplace. First you will see a definition of sexual harassment. Then, you will probably find a statement that looks something like this:

The *American Corporation* urges and encourages its employees to report incidents of sexual harassment. Reasonable effort will be made to protect the privacy of the complainant, the accused harasser, and all witnesses. Any employee who threatens an individual for the reporting of sexual harassment by retaliation, intimidation, or reprisal will be disciplined to the fullest extent.

The *American Corporation* will investigate all complaints of sexual harassment for the purpose of taking corrective action, when appropriate. If you believe you have been sexually harassed:

- Inform the alleged harasser of the sexual harassment conduct and/or
- Report the sexual harassment conduct to your supervisor or assigned agent.

Following the investigation of a sexual harassment complaint, the *American Corporation* will inform both parties of its conclusions. If an employee is found to have participated in sexual harassment, sanctions may be imposed, up to and including discharge.

This is a dummy complaint procedure. Your company will have its own bill of particulars, but the three essential areas formalized are:

- How to identify sexual harassment.
- How to report sexual harassment.
- How to monitor sexual harassment.

As we have shown throughout this book, however, procedures are just the beginning. *Knowing* the right thing to do is no guarantee that people will *do* the right thing in the throes of a conflict. We all have personal resistances that stop us from taking action each step of the way. People are often unaware of the roadblocks they erect that disable them from using the policy to help themselves.

Accordingly, in these final pages, it is our task to enrich your knowledge of the steps to take in response to sexual harassment with your knowledge of yourself. We will ask you to:

🕊 *Know the rules.* Review the steps to identify, report, and monitor sexual harassment.

🕊 *Know yourself.* Identify your resistances to using company policy on sexual harassment.

🕊 *Connect knowing and doing.* Reduce the gap between knowing the rules and knowing yourself.

This discussion is a practical field manual for *all* employees — those who are harassed, their managers, coworkers, and executives.

STEP 1
HOW TO IDENTIFY
SEXUAL HARASSMENT

The first requirement in traditional training is knowing how to identify sexual harassment. We will review the conditions that define it and that have been illustrated throughout this book in the dramatizations of Crystal and Liz.

Know the Rules

Federal law identifies two forms of sexual harassment. The first is quid pro quo sexual harassment. It occurs when submission to sexual favors is used as a condition of employment. An employee who is subjected to quid pro quo sexual harassment must show that:

- **Sexual advances** or requests for sexual favors are **unwelcome.**

- Sexual favors are demanded in **exchange** for favorable treatment or continued employment.

- Such conduct has the purpose or effect of substantially interfering with the individual's **work performance.**

Quid pro quo is also called supervisor sexual harassment. It has decreased in reported frequency (if not also occurrence) in the United States over the past decade. This may be a result of stricter laws, increased employee awareness, and potentially stiff penalties attached to the harassing supervisor and his or her employer. Moreover, because it is defined in part by the formal relationship between the protagonists, it is easier to spot.

Hostile, environment sexual harassment is the second form identified by federal law. It occurs when one employee harasses another employee because of his or her sex to the point at which the working environment becomes hostile. An employee who is subjected to a hostile work environment must show that:

The harassing conduct would not occur but for the employee's **gender.**

The harassing conduct is **severe or pervasive.**

A **reasonable person** would judge it so.

The conditions of employment are altered and the **work environment is hostile.**

Hostile environment sexual harassment, unlike quid pro quo is not decreasing in reported frequency in the United States. National estimates suggest the reverse trend. Awareness training has not significantly helped reduce these complaints.

The **boldfaced** terms shown in the definitions of quid pro quo and hostile environment sexual harassment are explained more fully in a glossary at the end of this appendix. These are the facts you need to know to help identify what is and is not sexual harassment. Does this help you to protect yourself? The real difficulty is in overcoming the personal resistances that get in the way of using what you know when called on to make decisions about workplace behavior.

Know Yourself

Make up a story about this picture. There are no right or wrong answers. Tell what you think could be going on and what the characters are thinking and feeling. Just make sure that your story has a beginning, middle, and an end.

Richard has been accused by Crystal of sexual harassment.

_____

_____

_____

_____

_____

_____

Appendix

SELF-ASSESSMENT

The story you have written is your starting point to gain insight into your potential roadblocks to using what you know to identify sexual harassment in your workplace. Although we cannot interpret your individual results, we can offer some general comments to guide your self-assessment. Based on review of many stories in response to this same picture, we have identified the critical issues that most people address in interpreting the picture. Compare your story to those we discuss now.

The picture shows Richard leaning closely over Crystal and the caption states, "Richard has been accused by Crystal of sexual harassment." The posture of the protagonists in the picture makes the caption believable. You have learned the definition of sexual harassment. Now let's see what you focus on when you interpret the picture.

The critical question for self-assessment is how do you depict Crystal and Richard? Score Crystal and Richard as you have presented them in your story, using the categories defined next. To help you decide in which category your depiction of Crystal or Richard best fits, we will show you several examples of stories from each category so you can compare yours to others in that group. At the end, we will interpret what your scores imply about how you view sexual harassment.

THE PROFILE OF A VICTIM

To begin your self-assessment, score your depiction of Crystal using a three-point scale. Assign Crystal a score of:

(1) If she is clearly being sexually harassed by Richard.

(2) If she is uncertain or confused about the sexual harassment.

(3) If she is misconstruing the sexual harassment.

Score 1: Crystal is "it"!

These are examples of a frankly sexually harassed Crystal:

> *Richard has come over to Crystal's desk to ask her a question. Crystal becomes uncomfortable with Richard leaning over her back. When he asks her what kind of underwear she prefers, she becomes very upset and offended. When he tries to explain he is buying an anniversary gift for his wife and wanted to know if women like wearing thong underwear, because women sure do look good in them, she becomes even more offended and accuses him of sexual harassment.*

> *Richard leans forward to get a closer look at the document on Crystal's desk. He catches a whiff of her shampoo or conditioner that he mistakes for perfume and thinks how nice she smells. She feels that he is invading her space, although he is maintaining a professional tone in his conversation.*

> *Crystal is working on a report at her desk. Unannounced and uninvited, Richard finds an opportunity to intrude and offer advice. Always bending over, always coming closer, and closer, and closer.*

This group of stories describes Crystal's adverse reaction to Richard's sexual harassment acts.

Score 2: Never mind!

These are examples of a tentative Crystal:

> *Richard appears to be giving instructions or listening to a question. Crystal seems to be insecure for some reason. The look on her face, her hair hanging down. Is this inexperience or immaturity? Of course, if you want to make trouble, you could ask the question, where is his other hand? What is he saying to her? Does she look like that because she is embarrassed? Only they know!*

> *The gentleman is leaning over to observe what Crystal is doing. She may feel awkward because she is not facing him or maintaining any eye contact. Perhaps she feels he has invaded her private space while he is simply trying to see what she is doing in a relaxed manner.*

> *She probably feels some discomfort because of his positioning over her. Maybe a threatening approach, if you don't like the person. However, the scene looks rather innocent to me. He is checking up on her tasks.*

This group of stories describes Crystal's uncertainty about Richard's suspect behavior.

Score 3: Will the real victim please step forward?

These are examples of a two-faced Crystal:

Richard asked Crystal to perform a certain task. He knows she won't do it correctly from past experience so he leans over her desk to watch her closely. She is uncomfortable with her boss looking over her shoulder. Crystal remembers the sexual harassment seminar she just went to and gets a good idea . . .

Crystal is a questionable performer, possibly in a new position. She feels threatened by her supervisor and uncomfortable with close scrutiny of her work. Richard is probably not a great manager. He involved himself in the day-to-day work instead of confronting a performance issue. Most of the time he avoids direct answers and hard questions.

This group of stories describes Crystal's deliberate misconstruction of Richard's actions.

Now turn to your story. How is your Crystal portrayed? Is Richard sexually harassing her? Or is the harassment denied or explained away? Do you disregard, blame, or empathize with Crystal?

THE PROFILE OF A SEXUAL HARASSER

As you did with Crystal, now score your depiction of Richard on a three-point scale. Assign Richard a score of:

(1) If he is clearly sexually harassing Crystal.

(2) If he is unintentional in his sexual harassment of Crystal.

(3) If he is wrongly accused by Crystal of sexual harassment.

Score 1: The phantom strikes!

These are examples of a frankly sexually harassing Richard:

Richard is instructing Crystal how to proceed on a project. In the process, he's using sexual innuendo to describe what he'd like her to do.

Infringement upon "territory" when not necessary. Behavior by Richard suggests domineering attitude and/or control, sexually or otherwise.

Crystal's demeanor indicates fear and a resignation that she has to bear Richard's overtures in order to keep her job.

Richard is supposed to be giving her instruction about how to run the computer. However, he is whispering sexually offending comments to her. She is offended by his remarks, but he is her boss. She has been told that if any of this is told to anyone, she will not receive any promotion.

Late at night. She is trying to work. He is flirting with her and asking her to go out with him. She feels put upon and tells him to back off. He cannot control himself and keeps flirting.

This group of stories describes Richard's hostile acts to an entrapped Crystal.

Score 2: "It was just a joke!"

These are examples of a misunderstood Richard:

> *Richard has learned of Crystal's accusation and is try-ing to explain to her that he meant no harm by his com-ments to her and he can't believe that she has accused him of sexual harassment. Crystal is unsure of how to react to him. She is trying to ignore him and continue with her work.*
>
> *Richard is trying to explain to Crystal that he didn't mean it. Leaning over her, he is acting like he cares.*
>
> *Crystal had been hired as the personal assistant of Richard more than three years ago. Her first job was of unusual importance to her, hence her willingness to work overtime with enthusiasm. For Richard, Crystal was the perfect right hand—swift, accurate, always there when needed. It would appear that on one occa-sion, Richard's informal approach as he leant over Crystal to read the screen of the computer—his tie might have brushed her shoulder. He might have put his hand on her shoulder in a way.*

This group of stories pleads Richard's innocence to an over-sensitive Crystal.

Score 3: Poor Richard!

These are examples of a victimized Richard:

Richard just wanted Crystal to do a good job (which she wasn't doing). He got too involved in Crystal's project.

Richard has been notified of Crystal's complaint and he is ill-advised to lean so closely over her. I believe that his ambiguous physical position, while probably innocent, is very ill-advised under the circumstances. Given the present climate—a very different one than that in which obviously middle-aged Richard grew up—his stance leaves him vulnerable to Crystal, who is probably looking for an excuse for why she is not keeping up with her performance standards.

This group of stories describes Richard's vulnerability to a devious Crystal.

Now turn to your story. How is Richard portrayed? Is he sexually harassing Crystal? Or is the harassment denied or explained away? Do you blame, disregard, or empathize with Richard?

Connect Knowing and Doing

The way in which you interpret Crystal and Richard in this story is indicative of the feelings you have about sexual harassers and their victims. The story you write is a first impression and taps your immediate reaction. If you were asked to render a formal opinion on a real case, you would have much more information on which to base your thinking. As psychologists, however, we know from extensive research and treatment that your first impression is revealing of the feelings you bring to the reasoning process; and feelings color perception, especially when forming judgments about topics that are not "black and white."

Your story is a snapshot of the particular feelings you bring to the table. You gain an appreciation of your personal concerns and biases when you compare your story to others.

To start, as a general observation you may notice in scoring your story that the way in which you describe one of the harassment partners affects the way you depict the other. That is, if your Crystal earns a score of 3 she is probably playing opposite a Richard who is also 3.

This is what we meant earlier in the book when we coined the term "harassment couple." When we make judgments of sexual harassment, we are always looking at the behavior of *two* people. The inferences we draw about what motivates it are based on our observations of dynamics of the relationship between the parties and not on the personality of either the harasser or victim alone.

The interpretation you are provided next of your story characterization, though not definitive, is a starting point to encourage you to think about yourself in relation to sexual harassment.

INTERPRETATION

Look under the heading **Score 1, 2, or 3** below and learn what emotions color your perception of Crystal and Richard based on how you rate the characters in your story exercise. These are the same emotions you carry to the job when called on to make judgments about workplace interactions. Your story gives you a few clues about what feelings may interfere with effective reasoning and action in responding to a harassment problem.

THE CRYSTAL SCALE

The Crystal Scale measures your capacity to identify sexual harassment and your personal feelings about it. Both affect how you react to sexual harassment victims. Please look up your interpretation of Crystal in the categories below.

Score 1: Crystal is "it"!

If your story falls in this category, you probably have little internal conflict about your perceptions of sexual harassment. You are secure in your capacity to read cues, infer intentions, and form judgments about the behavior of others in the workplace. Because of these capacities, you are quick to identify sexual harassment. To get an indication of your feelings toward sexual harassment victims, however, consider the emotions you attribute to Crystal. While she knows she is being harassed, is she angry? Intimidated? Reluctant to act? While you may know sexual harassment when you see it, do your feelings get in the way of taking effective action?

Score 2: Never mind!

If your story falls in this category, you are probably not one to jump to conclusions, especially if other people are involved. You prefer to think before you act. This may be because you doubt your judgment, are uncomfortable being the center of attention, or need to be certain you are "correct" before rendering an opinion. You "know" that Crystal has a problem, but are either afraid or unwilling to risk going with your intuition. You may, therefore, be more hesitant to identify sexual harassment, if it occurs. To get an indication of your feelings toward sexual harassment victims, however, consider the emotions you attribute to Crystal. Is she afraid of hurting Richard? Of being wrong? Of being ostracized by her coworkers? What holds Crystal back from making a decision about Richard's conduct?

Score 3: Will the real victim please step forward?

If your story falls in this category, you are probably skeptical about conventional conceptions of sexual harassment. You may know "chapter and verse" on the do's and don'ts and be compliant to your company's rules, but below the surface, you are an independent thinker. This is not to say you condone sexual harassment, but only that you have your own ideas about it. No amount of preaching policy will easily change your mind. To get an indication of your feelings toward sexual harassment victims, however, consider the emotions you attribute to Crystal. What is her motivation to wrongly accuse Richard? Is she manipulative and conniving, or desperate and pathetic? Would you feel the same if the gender of the protagonists in the story were reversed?

THE RICHARD SCALE

The Richard Scale measures your ability to recognize workplace aggression in others and your capacity for self-control. Both affect how you react to sexual harassers. Look under the heading **Score 1, 2, or 3** below, just as you did for Crystal. Find out what emotions color your perceptions based on how you rate Richard in your story exercise.

Score 1: *The phantom strikes!*

If your story falls in this category, you probably have good intuition and recognize hostility for what it is, whether veiled or overt. You have good instincts and can "see it coming." Because of these capacities, you have little trouble identifying harassment behavior. To get an indication of your feelings toward sexual harassers, however, consider the emotions you attribute to Richard. Is he a villain? Do you fear him? Is he a buffoon? Do you feel sorry for him? Knowing Richard may not help you protect yourself from him. Your reaction to his hostility also predicts if you are a likely candidate for his harassment behavior.

Score 2: *It was just a joke!*

If your story falls in this category, you are probably uncomfortable dealing with aggression, yours or that of other people. You strive to neutralize any show of hostility, perhaps to ward off feeling helpless, threatened or out of control. While you may do this to protect yourself, it also leaves you vulnerable to engagement in a harassment entanglement. To get an indication of your feelings toward sexual harassers, however, consider the emotions you attribute to Richard. Is he in denial? Is he in a rage? Is his hostility disguised as seduction? What could you do to discover what Richard is really all about? Backing off does not stop Richard, nor does it protect you.

Score 3: *Poor Richard!*

If your story falls in this category, you probably have significant difficulty dealing with aggression. You may also have a personal history that is marked by confusion about how to constructively express your anger in a way that is helpful to your situation. In your story, you negate Richard's hostility and reinvent him as the "victim" of Crystal's aggression. This way of turning around emotions leaves you prone to the kinds of misinterpretations that typify harassment relationships. To get an indication of your feelings toward sexual harassers, however, consider the emotions you attribute to Richard. Is he resentful and self-pitying? Or is he vulnerable and unprotected? What makes him prey to Crystal? When aggression is defended against this strongly, a door is left ajar for interpersonal problems to develop on the job.

S T E P 2
H O W   T O   R E P O R T
S E X U A L   H A R A S S M E N T

Know the Rules

Most corporations have a policy that specifies what sexual harassment is, to whom it should be reported, and who is responsible for correcting it. The situation for quid pro quo harassment is unambiguous. As we have shown, its definition is straightforward and employer liability is absolute. If adverse tangible action results from a supervisor's harassing conduct, whether or not the employer has notice of it, the corporation is held liable.

For hostile environment sexual harassment, the actions of the victim have more bearing on the outcome of the problem. Employer liability is not absolute. The Supreme Court demands of the employer that it exercise reasonable care to prevent and promptly correct any conduct constituting sexual harassment; and of the harassed employee, that he or she take advantage of personnel policy or procedure to report or correct sexually harassing conduct before turning outside the corporation for help.

Based on these guidelines, harassed employees, their managers, and executive officers are all called on to act on behalf of stopping hostile environment sexual harassment. Just as the corporation has had to assume greater accountability to protect employees from harassment, so have victims had to assume greater responsibility to alert the employer of a harassment problem. If, without cause, a harassed employee fails to use the corporation's policy and procedure to stop the harassment, the employer may have an affirmative defense.

These new guidelines put all employees on notice. We strongly urge you to read your company's policy and learn what is your obligation to your employer in cases of sexual harassment.

American workers feel the impact of the new laws. The national swell of complaints of coworker harassment attests to this. People are more inclined to come forward and report. This is the endpoint of the traditional treatment of sexual harassment. A problem is identified, it is reported, investigated, and depending on the finding, the accused is sanctioned.

Then what? Is the problem ended?

"Punishing" accused harassers, as we have shown throughout this book, does little to promote positive change—in either the harassment protagonists or in the company. Let's take a look at what gets unleashed when the endpoint of the harassment treatment is reaching a finding on the wrongdoing.

Know Yourself

Make up a story about this picture. There are no right or wrong answers. Tell what you think could be going on and what Crystal is thinking and feeling. Just make sure that your story has a beginning, middle, and an end.

Crystal receives an important call.

Self-Assessment

The story you have written to the picture is your starting point to promote thought about your expectations of what will happen once sexual harassment is reported. These feelings affect how you make decision about what to do in the workplace.

Identified as harassment "victim" in the first exercise, Crystal is shown in this next picture talking privately on the telephone. The caption reads, "Crystal receives an important call." The exercise taps your feelings about reporting sexual harassment. What happens to Crystal *after* the news of the harassment is "let out"? Is she helped or hurt further?

The critical question for self-assessment is what is the outcome of Crystal's action?

Score your story using the category guidelines defined below, as you did before. To help you decide in which category your response belongs, we show you several examples of Crystal stories from each group so you can compare yours to others. At the end, we interpret what your score implies about how you view the consequences of exposing sexual harassment on the victim.

The consequences for exposing sexual harassment

To begin your self-assessment, score your outcome of Crystal's action using a three-point scale. Assign a score of:

(1) If dire consequences,

(2) If insufficient action,

(3) If appropriate help,

results from Crystal's action to expose Richard's harassment of her.

Score 1: Dire consequences.

A group of responses falls in this category that differ in accordance to *who* is the target of retaliation.

Crystal is the most frequent choice:

She is fired!

This picture tells us that Crystal is not elated with her news. I doubt very much this is a personal call! She has a highly concerned look on her face and appears worried. I feel confident it is a call that her job is no longer hers.

Crystal, we will be transferring you out of the department.

Crystal receives a call from the police. Richard has been murdered and she is a suspect.

Sometimes the misfortune falls on Richard's shoulders:

Richard calls Crystal to apologize for his action. He says he did not mean to harm or upset her. Crystal is sad and wants to cry because now she knows the two will always be uncomfortable working together. Crystal considers quitting but then decides to get even with Richard and begins a campaign of public humiliation of Richard. The end.

Crystal holds the telephone receiver in her hand and contemplates her false charges against her supervisor as a desperate plea for attention.

Still less often, the employer "takes the hit":

Crystal is receiving a call from her lawyer, whom she has called to help her through this problem. After getting no satisfaction from her supervisor at the company, she has taken it the legal route. The company now has to enter a class action sexual harassment suit brought on by Crystal.

No matter who is the target of retaliation—Crystal, Richard, or the corporation—all of the stories in this group share a common depiction of a bitter consequence to Crystal's decision to expose the sexual harassment. Interestingly, this is the *largest* category of responses in our sample.

Score 2: A ray of hope . . .

In these stories, Crystal wages a fight-back but is facing a difficult or losing battle:

Doesn't look like good news . . . it's her word against his.

Crystal receives a call from Richard's boss. He is very gentle with her, but is also patronizing. Her position is secure, but she comes to realize during the conversation that her complaint is not taken seriously. She will continue to work with Richard. She is encouraged to discuss any future complaints with Richard's boss, but she is also gently warned that the complaints should be of a more serious nature. If she complains about insubstantial matters, it could reflect badly on her.

The phone call is from Richard's boss asking Crystal to come into his office. She appears quite scared by the party on the line and most definitely disappointed in what is being said to her. The sadness in her face suggests that she may be fired or transferred out of the department.

Crystal is concentrating. Since we do not know who the call is from, she is speaking into the telephone receiver—not open to the rest of the office. If it is regarding the complaint, maybe she is thinking she got a senior person into trouble or the person on the phone is challenging her.

These stories depict an outcome to exposing the sexual harassment that is a notch more hopeful than before. Though threatened with retaliation, this Crystal still has a chance of fair treatment. This is the *second largest* category of responses in our sample.

Score 3: The cavalry arrives!

In these stories, Crystal gets appropriate help:

You should come to personnel immediately!

Richard's boss calls Crystal and assures her that action has been taken. She will now report to a different manager. Crystal is embarrassed but relieved that she was heard.

This may be a call from her boss, asking for a formal explanation and informing Crystal of her options. It may be a call from Richard, her attorney, a friend she has confided in, another accuser? The most important call, I believe, would be one which explains her rights objectively. If she is particularly distressed, a call offering sympathy and friendship may be equally important, as a prelude to a more formal conversation.

The boss calls Crystal and tells her that if Richard should exhibit any further harassment toward her she should report this to management immediately. Crystal is relieved that the boss took her complaint seriously.

This is the *smallest* category of responses in our sample!

Now look back and re-read your story. Where do you find yourself? What does this imply about your expectations of your employer to "do the right thing" if you stick your neck out and take a stand against sexual harassment?

Connect Knowing and Doing

The way in which you interpret Crystal in this story is indicative of the feelings you have about the consequences to the victim for exposing sexual harassment. Emotions color perception and therefore affect how you might react were you to find yourself in a similar situation. Therefore the insight you gain from self-assessment prepares you to be more effective if you or someone you know is being sexually harassed.

INTERPRETATION

This exercise measures your trust in the employer to respond affirmatively to the victims of sexual harassment and your personal feelings about reaching out to others in the corporation to solve a harassment problem. Both of these come into play when making a decision about reporting or otherwise acting on sexual harassment.

Look under the heading **Score 1, 2, or 3** below and learn what emotions color your perception of the consequences of exposing sexual harassment based on how you rate Crystal's outcome in this story. These are the same emotions you carry to the job when called on to make a decision about what to do. Your story gives you a few clues about what feelings may interfere with you taking effective action in response to a harassment problem.

Score 1: Dire consequences.

If your story falls in this category, you probably have little faith in the employer to respond empathically or affirmatively to sexual harassment victims. Fear of retribution is a powerful deterrent to reporting, no matter what procedural guarantees are available to prohibit retaliation. You may be quite skeptical about the outcome of "blowing the whistle" even if you believe intellectually and morally that it is the right thing to do. To get an indication, however, of your personal feelings about reaching out to others to share the harassment problem, consider the emotions you attribute to Crystal. How does she respond to the "bad news"? Is she passive? Worried? Angry? Rageful? Negative anticipation about the reactions you will receive from others can stop you from taking effective action, just as can distrust in your employer.

Score 2: A ray of hope . . .

If your story falls in this category, you are probably guarded, though willing to take a chance on the employer to respond affirmatively to sexual harassment victims. Shored up by your confidence in your judgment and interpretation of the sexual harassment events, conviction overrides doubt, though you are uncertain of what lies ahead. To get an indication, however, of your personal feelings about reaching out to others for support, consider the emotions you attribute to Crystal. Is she disappointed in the response she receives from the person on the other end of the telephone? Is she intimidated by the response? Or is she a martyr to the cause? Your feelings affect whether or not you turn to others in the workplace to help solve a harassment problem, as does degree of trust in your employer.

Score 3: The cavalry arrives!

If your story falls in this category, you probably trust the employer to respond affirmatively to sexual harassment victims. This trust is often based on positive experiences in your personal history when you have known or worked for employers with genuine concern for employees in the organization. Alternatively, if your story is to "rosy," wake up! No case of sexual harassment is resolved without some blood, sweat, and tears.

To get an indication, however, of your personal feelings about reaching out to others when you need help, consider the emotions you attribute to Crystal. Is she appropriately conflicted? Is she relieved, but also regretful? Or is she lacking in empathy for the accused? Even if the employer is deemed trustworthy, your feelings about seeking help will also affect how likely you are to use the parachute provided to the victims of sexual harassment.

STEP 3
HOW TO MONITOR
SEXUAL HARASSMENT

Know the Rules

It falls to leadership in the corporation to see to it that the workplace atmosphere is free of gender based hostility in all its forms. At a minimum, this means that the employer must have and monitor an anti-harassment policy and complaint procedure, and provide training to employees on how to identify and respond to sexual harassment.

We have reviewed the definitions of what constitutes sexual harassment. We have reviewed the necessary steps to follow if you or someone you know is being sexually harassed. We have spoken at length about emotions and resistances that pose roadblocks to effective self-advocacy, including those you may have toward victims, harassers, or relying on the help of coworkers.

Now it is time to focus attention on the employer. Just having a policy "on the books" isn't enough. The employer must also routinely check that it is effective, that employees have access to it, and that they understand how to use it. Practically speaking, in most corporations Human Resources is assigned the task of monitoring compliance and hearing employee disputes.

We urge you to find out who in your place of employment is responsible for resolving problems in employee relations, including sexual harassment. This is shown in your company's antiharassment policy.

In the last exercise we looked at trust in the employer to act affirmatively on behalf of the victims of sexual harassment. We now broaden the question to include confidence in the employer to safeguard the workplace environment for the benefit of *all* employees—not just to rectify the wrongs committed against the few victims of sexual harassment. How deep is the employer's commitment to create and maintain a workplace that is free of discrimination?

Know Yourself

Make up a story about this picture. There are no right or wrong answers. Tell what you think could be going on and what the characters are thinking and feeling. Just make sure that your story has a beginning, middle, and an end.

The boss discusses the sexual harassment complaint with Richard.

_____

_____

_____

_____

_____

_____

_____

Appendix

_____

_____

_____

_____

_____

_____

_____

_____

_____

_____

_____

_____

_____

_____

_____

_____

_____

_____

_____

SELF-ASSESSMENT

The story you have written to the picture is your starting point to explore your level of trust in the employer to monitor the workplace for hostility. In the last exercise, you saw what happened to Crystal in the harassment aftermath. Now let's see what happens to Richard. The picture in this exercise shows him sitting opposite the desk from his boss. The caption reads, "The boss discusses the sexual harassment complaint with Richard."

This exercise taps your feelings about whether you can rely on leadership to protect your rights. When sexual harassment is uncovered "all eyes are on the boss." Whether out in the open or behind closed doors, the accuser, the accused, and coworkers all wait anxiously to see what leadership is going to do to correct the problem. It is therefore a critical time in the recovery of the organization. The actions taken by the leader can build or bust employee trust.

The critical question for self-assessment is how does the boss react to Richard?

Score your story using the categories defined next. To help you decide in which category your response belongs, we show you several examples of stories from each group so you can compare yours to others. At the end, we interpret what your score implies about your level of confidence in the corporation to monitor sexual harassment effectively.

RECOVERY STARTS AT THE TOP

To begin your self-assessment, score the boss using a three-point scale. Assign a score of:

(1) If the boss is guilty of foul play.

(2) If the boss denies the events are sexual harassment.

(3) If the boss takes appropriate action.

Score 1: "The fish stinks from the head!"

In these stories, the boss colludes with Richard in cold-blooded violation of Crystal's rights:

> "Hey Dick. Crystal is saying that you keep bugging her, want to go out with her. Since she's not cooperative why not hit on someone else? We don't need any trouble here."

> Richard let his boss know of the potential complaints. They agreed that for the good of the company, they would remove the source of the problem—namely Crystal. They then beat a hasty retreat to the nearest watering hole for a scotch.

> They may look like they're taking it seriously but they will have a "good old boy" talk afterward and laugh a little.

A variation on this theme, the boss ditches the trouble-maker Richard:

> Richard and Crystal's supervisor has just 38 months to go until he is 59½ and can start withdrawing funds from his 401(k) plan. He decides that Richard must be sacrificed on the altar of Political Correctness.

Not much interpretation is needed for these stories. Not only is trust lacking in leadership, but management is actually seen as pointedly malevolent or self-serving. The only unexpected twist is that the frequency of this story category is the *highest* in our sample of respondents, for both men and women.

Score 2: The ostrich.

In these stories, this boss is less malevolent but still in denial about the sexual harassment:

> *Richard is surprised by what his boss is telling him. He has always been friendly with his secretaries, giving them flowers on Secretary's Day, taking them out for lunch or drinks. He thinks this young girl must be a "Woman's Libber." His boss says that confidentially, of course, he agrees with Richard, but that the "Old Timers" have to pay lip service to these young whipper-snappers because they are close to retirement and have their pensions at stake.*

> *They look as if they are in agreement—"brotherhood." Very casual. Boss shows little concern. Neither he nor Richard seems surprised by the allegations.*

> *Richard: "I tell you boss, my friendly attitude toward Crystal has been misunderstood. I have never come on to her." Boss: Crystal probably has some basis for her claim but Richard seems sincere. I wish this whole mess would go away. They're making a mountain out of a molehill.*

Richard and his boss are agreeing that Crystal's accusations are unimportant and probably stem from misunderstanding.

Unlike the boss's outright collusion with Richard shown before, this time he does not dismiss the sexual harassment events entirely. However, in denying the seriousness of the problem, he hides his head in the sand and fails to protect Crystal, help Richard, or shield the corporation from harm. Incidentally, this is the *second* most frequent story category told by our sample, falling only modestly behind the first group.

Score 3: Mopping up the mess.

There are a number of spins on the good boss theme, though overall it is the lowest frequency category in our sample of respondents.

Some stories depict a *confident* boss confronting Richard:

The boss is taking this seriously, being straight, honest. Richard is not believing his boss, based on disbelief posture. The boss continues anyway.

Richard learns from his boss that his behavior was WRONG. He is willing to work to change.

Others depict a *protective* boss defending Crystal:

Richard's boss discusses Crystal's perception of her relationship with Richard, and tells him to watch himself in the future.

Fewer, though a significant number, envision an *impartial* boss who sees the problem from all sides:

> *Richard is surprised to learn of the complaint. His boss explains the situation and Richard listens intently. He learns that he should respect Crystal's personal space. His boss tells him that if he wants to keep his job he will have to respect Crystal's wishes and for the moment he is being moved to a different office.*

> *I am assuming Richard and his boss have not discussed this issue before. Richard is likely to feel embarrassment, shame, and confusion. He may be angry if he feels wrongly accused. Whether or not he feels guilty, he is likely to feel afraid of his corporate and legal positions, and will probably attempt to make excuses or "play down" the accusation. Richard's boss may be confused with respect to his obligations. His response will depend on what type of person he is, how well informed he is on this matter, and how well he knows both individuals involved. A good boss will deal with this matter as objectively and fairly as possible.*

Now look back and re-read your story. Where do you find yourself? Do you fall in one of the three categories outlined? What does this imply about your level of confidence in the employer to protect the work environment against hostility and intimidation?

Appendix

Connect Knowing and Doing

The way in which you interpret the boss in relation to Richard in this story is indicative of the feelings you have about trusting authority in your organization to safeguard the environment against discrimination. Emotions color perception and therefore affect how you might react were you find yourself in a harassment situation. We encourage you to think about your expectations of leadership to control the threat of workplace hostility.

INTERPRETATION

This exercise measures your confidence in your employer to safeguard the environment against sexual harassment and your level of trust in authority figures to be fair in their treatment of you. You need both to feel secure in your workplace, especially after sexual harassment has been alleged.

Look under the heading **Score 1, 2,** or **3** and learn what emotions color your perception of leadership based on how you rate the boss in his treatment of the Richard problem. These are the same emotions you carry to the job when called on to make a decision about who you can trust in a harassment situation or to rebuild trust in your employer after sexual harassment has occurred.

Score 1: The fish stinks from the head!

If your story falls into this category you probably have a dim view of leadership and do not trust your employer to create a safe workplace. You may be reluctant to rely on anyone in the corporation to assist you in the matter of sexual harassment, no matter the availability of Human Resource specialists with well-formulated policies. This may be because you have had negative experiences with authority figures in your personal history. Alternatively, you may not be a person who easily establishes trust. In either event, re-read your story and note the manner in which good faith was violated. By whom? The particular way in which trust was broken may have special meaning to you.

Score 2: The ostrich.

If your story falls into this category, you are probably skeptical of leadership and uncertain if it can be trusted to be impartial in protecting employee rights. But you have not given up all hope. Your boss does keep an open ear, if not an open mind to Richard. Analyzing your story once more, what holds the boss back from successful resolution of the problem? Does he place equal value on both partners in the harassment couple? Or does his preferential treatment of one over the other sound an alarm throughout the organization that bias is tolerated? Looking at it yet another way, is the boss self-serving and indifferent to employee problems altogether? How does the boss's attitude affect coworkers who are not directly involved in the sexual harassment, but who have been silent observers? The way in which you depict the boss may be revealing of why your confidence in leadership to be fair-minded is limited.

Score 3: Mopping up the mess.

If your story falls into this category, you have probably given a good deal of thought to "all sides of the elephant" when considering the problem of sexual harassment. You may be open to using the resources of the corporation if need arises because you can imagine a benign leadership that can take affirmative action and protect the rights of all parties involved. Analyzing your story once more, however, is the boss in conflict when confronting Richard? If you have painted a too rosy picture of this meeting, wake up! Denying the emotions of the boss in the harassment aftermath creates a blind spot in protecting yourself from disappointment when you discover that everyone—even an enlightened boss—brings personal feelings to the table when negotiating harassment problems.

PUTTING IT ALL TOGETHER

Throughout this book we have endeavored to "slow the speedboat" of sexual harassment in order to demonstrate how it develops above and below the horizon of awareness, and hopefully alter its course before it hits you or someone you know. To do this we analyzed the case study of Richard, Crystal, and Liz, and invited you to explore your own feelings about sexual harassment through the self-assessment exercises. By continually rotating your lens of observation, we hope you have gotten a glimmer of insight into the many emotions you bring to the reasoning process when it comes to interpreting sexual harassment.

Does all this help? We offer no quick cures to sexual harassment. The motivations behind it are complex and deeply embedded. To promise cultural change on so grand a scale by any one training experience is to hawk fool's gold. If nothing else is apparent from this book, we hope we have impressed upon you that you carry a unique combination of emotions and life experiences that bias your thinking in special ways. To believe you can be neutral in applying a set of workplace rules is only to fool yourself.

The first challenge in prevention is to know which of your biases is likely to influence you when you are called on to respond to sexual harassment. This is true if you find yourself in the seat of the harassed, the accused harasser, the colleague onlooker, the responsible manager, or the executive policymaker.

This completes the self-assessment. You have taken a glimpse in the mirror to see the emotions and perceptions you bring to the task of understanding sexual harassment. We fully recognize however, that no one glance gives you the whole picture of yourself. That ambitious a goal we dare not set for ourselves with only this limited opportunity of self-assessment.

But you have had a good beginning. We hope you can appreciate the complexities of sexual harassment and respect that the feelings you have about it are as important to understand as are the rules and policies your company has to prohibit it.

GLOSSARY

Gender: In hostile environment sexual harassment, the discriminatory conduct must have occurred *because* of the victim's sex. This means that the offensive conduct would not have occurred otherwise but for his or her gender.

In exchange for: Quid pro quo sexual harassment occurs when an employer attempts to make an employee submit to sexual demands *as a condition of his or her employment.* Refusal by the employee may be because of threatened or actual retaliation by the employer in the form of loss of tangible benefits or denial of future opportunities. Termination from the job, unfavorable performance review, pass-over for promotion, or loss of salary are among the more common reprisals threatened by harassing employers.

Interfere with work performance: In quid pro quo sexual harassment, the victim must demonstrate that the complained-of conduct seriously affected personal *well being* or *capacity to perform at work.* Among the common types of personal injury claimed is *psychological distress.* This can take many forms, including depression, anxiety, loss of appetite, and insomnia, which can diminish capacity to function in the workplace.

Reasonable person: In hostile environment sexual harassment, judgments of severity and pervasiveness of complained-of conduct must be considered from the perspective of a *reasonable person.* Would a *typical employee* be offended by the conduct? Some states have modified this standard to that of a *reasonable person of the same gender* as the complainant. This modification acknowledges that men and women have unique perspectives on what constitutes offensive conduct, and these gender differences should be considered in making judgments about sexual harassment.

Severe or pervasive: In hostile environment sexual harassment, it is the *harassing conduct* that must be severe or pervasive, not its *effect* on the complainant. A single, severe act of discrimination may constitute harassment, or many independent acts can collectively constitute harassment. Inclusion of both criteria is based on the finding that complainants typically report numerous incidents of unwelcome conduct, which, if considered individually, might *not* be considered sufficiently *severe*. But when considered together, these offenses may be sufficiently *pervasive* to make the environment abusive and intimidating.

Sexual advance: A broad range of behaviors may be considered as sexual advances, only some of which are strictly *sexual* in nature. Acts such as offensive verbal remarks, propositions, comments which are gender-based, visual acts such as leering or displaying lewd pictures, physical acts such as touching and fondling, or finally explicit sexual contact may all be considered as sexual harassment.

Unwelcome: An advance that is unwanted and uninvited is *unwelcome*. Employees who receive such advances often go along with it because of fear, intimidation, or the perception of punishment or reprisal in the event of refusal. In such cases, *submission* does not necessarily imply *consent*, and the advance must be viewed in the context of the circumstances which surround it.

Work environment is hostile: In hostile environment sexual harassment, complained-of conduct must be sufficiently severe or pervasive to alter the conditions of employment and create an abusive environment. A hostile environment may be created for an employee *even if the harassment conduct was not directed to that employee.* That is, if an employee's coworker is the target, the environment may nonetheless be abusive to others who are indirectly exposed.

INDEX